Praise for *The Book of Tiny Prayer*

"Just as one tiny speck of glitter lights up an entire face, each of these radiant tiny prayers sparkles with huge hope. They are jewels of honest introspection, poetic gifts born of a year of turmoil, collected as a trail of glitter crumbs, lighting up our way back home to the soul."

—Rabbi Amichai Lau-Lavie,
Founding Spiritual Leader of Lab/Shul

"Prayer changes things; this was central to my childhood faith training. And the older I get, the more the world turns in ways that cause me deep concern, the more I believe it to be true. These tiny prayers from Micah Bucey's big heart add up to something far larger than first meets the eye. In the midst of fear, grief, and continuing injustices, these are sincere expressions of the desire to dream God's dream, with the power to center us, comfort us, ground us, and galvanize us for the sacred work we must be doing in order to heal our souls and the world. This collection is a very specific record of a very specific year, but the sense of yearning and hope will inspire lives of love and justice for years to come."

—The Rev. Dr. Jacqui Lewis,
Senior Minister, Middle Collegiate Church, and
author, *Fierce Love: A B.......... ...ous Courage
...il the World*

The Book of Tiny Prayer

THE
BOOK
OF
TINY
PRAYER

DAILY

MEDITATIONS

FROM THE

PLAGUE YEAR

MICAH BUCEY

FORDHAM UNIVERSITY PRESS

NEW YORK

2022

Fordham University Press has no responsibility for
the persistence or accuracy of URLs for external
or third-party Internet websites referred to in this
publication and does not guarantee that any content
on such websites is, or will remain, accurate or
appropriate.

Fordham University Press also publishes its books
in a variety of electronic formats. Some content that
appears in print may not be available in electronic
books.

Visit us online at www.fordhampress.com.

Library of Congress Cataloging-in-Publication Data
available online at https://catalog.loc.gov.

Printed in the United States of America

24 23 22 5 4 3 2 1

First edition

For all question-askers,
transformation-seekers,
and change-makers

Contents

Foreword

I don't know Micah. I've never met him. A few years ago, I stood outside Judson Memorial Church one cold winter evening in New York, a time when the then-president was planning to deport Dreamers who had the right to remain. I stopped because of the bulletin board. *Let My People Stay* is what it said. I'd never heard of Judson. Who are these people? I wondered. I read four words that echoed a biblical sensibility, four words with a mix of play and fury in the *Stay*, and an unbudging assertion of belonging in the *My*.

I liked what I saw in those four words. But I still don't know Micah. I've met him in this book, though. And here's what I know: he's had Long Covid, he gets tired; he's queer, white, and powerful and sometimes feels powerless. He's guilty about the things that benefit him while burdening others, he's interested in art, he knows that small comforts from each other can help build a movement, he's got an interest in language and literature and delight. He has had suffering in his life. And he has love. He was held together by making small prayers on his phone throughout the strangest year. He's got huge requests. He's got humble ones. He knows he's not the answer, and he's not interested in dogmas that are too certain about what the answer is. These prayers are intimate, at times poetic, at times fumbling, at times in shock, at times unsure of what to say. In this way, I meet a man I like.

Who is Micah praying to? It's hard to know. He's cautious about naming any God, and these tiny prayers, casual as they sometimes are, nonetheless keep to this most strict of forms. In the face of Unknowing, he does not seek to name, to sound what he calls a "stationary noun." Instead, he wishes to lift up an "active verb." God is a *doing* in this book of prayers. Micah seeks evidence of this *doing* everywhere around. Cautious as he is about the names of God, Micah's happy to name many others. To list the names of people he prays for is like a litany, like old-time Bible genealogy: postal workers, farm workers, homeless people, incarcerated people; people facing unemployment, loneliness, shock; people who mother, people looking for their mothers; cities and people helping cities face their history; people wearing masks, people who refuse. These prayers are political, written during the final year of Donald Trump's presidency, written during the year of George Floyd's murder, written during the year of an election, during the year of a pandemic. The world that's revealed through these prayers is recognizable, not because it's fresh and new and awful but because it's old and aching and often awful. These are tiny prayers that do not turn away.

Micah prays by typing things into his phone. A world has a new vocabulary: Covid, masks, mandate, shelter-in-place, herd immunity, Astra Zeneca, lockdown. A world has an old vocabulary: privilege,

separation, discrimination, pleasure, pain,
indifference, oppression, exhaustion. The
man is writing tiny prayers—one every day.
Micah directs prayers toward the source
of goodness and change, hoping that the
people he names—himself among the
mix—might be the site of transformation,
reformation, honesty, reparation, and
delight. While he does not name a god, it is
clear where he finds one: in art, in people,
in justice, in movements toward truth
and solidarity, in bearing witness, in risk,
in honoring the dead: John Prine, David
Driskell, Dr. Lorna M. Breen, George Floyd,
Breonna Taylor, Ruth Bader Ginsburg,
Walter Wallace Jr., Cicely Tyson, Lawrence
Ferlinghetti.

Why does a person pray? The word
itself is an echo of French, *prier*, to ask.
The person praying is asking for things:
sometimes humble things, sometimes huge
things. The person is feeling helpless, even
amidst the privileges he knows he has. He
is reaching out beyond himself, writing
tiny prayers in this secular space. Another
French word, *secular*, also *siècle* meaning
century, meaning "face the world you're

in," meaning to be present in time. The
person is praying right where they are, in
a time of political, epidemiological, and
social crisis.

What is prayer for? It's hard to know.
If nothing else it is a repository of desire.
These prayers of Micah Bucey's are prayers
for. They're for space; and breath; and hope
and justice. They're for justice, revelation,
art, delight, spontaneity, and repentance.
They're for confession and contribution.
They're small—*tiny*, he calls them—and
he knows they're not going to change the
world, but he prays for a changed world
anyway.

On March 5, toward the end of a year of
these little prayers, Micah prays this:

For those who need to take a breath and, for just a moment, simply be

May you.

Amen

The title is five times longer than the
prayer. Isn't this often the way? Our many
words wish for something that words can't
contain, something small, something that

opens: a window, perhaps, or a door. Fresh air. Growth.

The word may is everywhere in these prayers, usually the first word. May you be, grow, change, lift, say, undo, do, he says. Say it. Shape the sound with your mouth. May. The word may starts with a hum. That mmm sound before the ay sound. A hum can be a song, can be an agreement, can be a sound of sympathy or shock. Mmm can be pleasure or an Amen. Before the mmm there needs to be a breath; the body needs air before it can make this noise of listening. So it always has been: before the first word, a breath, and in that breath, we hope there's life abundant. Micah prays for gasps of wonder too; an aaah to add to the mmmm. Amen, and all the sounds of being human.

Pádraig Ó Tuama,
the northern tip of Ireland,
August 2021

A Brief Introduction to Some Tiny Prayers, or The Longest Entry You'll Read in This Book

I have a complicated relationship with prayer.

Growing up the son of a Midwestern preacher man, I've been through my devout phase, my rebellious phase, my spiritual-but-not-religious phase, my somewhat reluctant return to church and seminary phase, and I've now landed in a space where my own life as a spiritual leader is mostly defined by lots of question-asking, creative improvisation, and openness to being changed. Through all these phases, prayer has been a constant, but prayer has also always felt both familiar and foreign, always potentially heartening but also always potentially harmful. I've been both encouraged to pray and told that I don't pray correctly. I've struggled to focus and wondered if I'm just talking to myself. As a queer person who has been told by more than one anti-queer "believer" that they "pray for" me, I have experienced how the idea of prayer can be wielded as a weapon to demean and degrade. As a person of curious faith who has run from and then tentatively tiptoed back toward spiritual community, I have witnessed how prayer can also be a radically healing act that invites us to step out of our hurried timelines, connect with a community and spirit larger than ourselves, and breathe into change and challenges with confidence and commitment.

I have been praying a lot lately.

Some of this praying has been done in private, but much of it has been done in public, through the 366 prayers that now make up this little collection. What you currently hold is a chronicle of where my own heart has traveled and where our world has traveled over the course of the first year of the COVID-19 pandemic. As I write this Introduction, many of the safety mandates that have been constant realities in our lives are being lifted. Masks are coming off. Vaccines are finding their way into more and more bodies. Hope is on the horizon. But much is still uncertain. New variants of the virus and new waves of infection are still snaking their way into certain populations. The buildup of unprocessed grief and trauma that lurks just beneath our skin is rearing its head in unpredictable ways. So much loss has left us wounded and stunned. The economic and racial inequalities baked into our systems continue to be shown in ever-starker light. There's a ton of things to pray about and there's a ton of individual and collective work to be done.

I didn't set out to write a book of prayers. But as the COVID-19 pandemic invaded all our lives, as social distancing pulled us apart, as space was left between us and fear filled the void, I found that I needed a practice that would help to lift me out of the overwhelm of the news, focus my attention and intention on one small thing I could address each day, and propel me to invite others to do this tiny, mindful action with me. From March 24, 2020, to March 24, 2021, I kept this practice of writing a "Tiny Prayer" each morning and posting it on social media, and, in addition to sustaining my own sanity through a year of pain and protest, it became an account of a moment in time, as messy, imperfect, and fragile as the most desperate, improvised prayers are.

I still remember the specific moment in time when the first of these "Tiny Prayers" popped out of my heart. It didn't come to me through formal silence. I wasn't quietly sitting, awaiting a sign from the divine. It came to me while I was going about my normal busy-ness in a rapidly changing landscape. My home, New York City, began to enter its lockdown phase on March 22, 2020, and even though non-essential workers were told to stay home, I had one task I felt compelled to complete before I cloistered myself behind my own apartment door. In my part-time work with a faith-based immigrant-rights organization, one of my roles was to deliver cashier's check bond payments to help release immigrant friends from

ICE detention. On March 24, even as so many stores and offices were closing, the immigration bond office at 26 Federal Plaza was still open, so I was determined to pay one more bond and get one more immigrant friend released before the entire city shut down. But there was a problem: I couldn't find an open bank.

As I rushed around the city, Googling the words "bank near me" and finding only darkened windows and "Temporarily Closed" signs, an alert came in on my phone screen: "Playwright Terrence McNally, 81, dies of coronavirus-related complications." I stopped in my tracks. It was the first celebrity death I'd noted since rumors of this pandemic had begun to dominate the news cycle, it was the death of a hero of mine, and it was the death of an artist who had not only survived another devastating plague (AIDS) but who had also, through a series of celebrated theater pieces, frankly and beautifully chronicled that moment in time, most especially the fear, grief, trauma, and resilience of a community who had refused to be silent or die without a fight.

Compelled by a combination of celebration for Mr. McNally's life, grief over his passing, and anxiety attached to the illness, loss, and alienation that was engulfing all our lives, I opened my Facebook app, typed the words "Today's Tiny Prayer (for Terrence McNally)," followed by twenty-three more words and an "Amen," and posted them. This first offering erupted from a place within me where I hadn't yet admitted to myself I needed to dwell, that place where honest fear and honest faith mingle and create something new; something hopeful, but not saccharine; something authentic, but not despairing; something like prayer.

The next day, I wrote and posted a prayer for healthcare workers, then the next day, one for faith leaders, then the next, one for those who were afraid. Each subsequent prayer grew organically from there. I began to get up each morning, check in with my own spirit and with that day's news, and then challenge myself to zoom in on one issue, refusing to get lost in the enormity of all that we were facing and deciding to respond to one piece of the puzzle at a time. Before I knew it, the practice was both automatic and a mode of survival.

As I continued to compose and post, another, somewhat unexpected gift began to blossom: People actually responded. I was invited into dozens of conversations with other seekers of various identities, including those who gladly call themselves "religious" or "spiritual," those who feel somewhat uncomfortable claiming those terms, and those who seek absolutely no association with those terms. Folks would reach out if a specific prayer resonated with them on a particular day. Many of them also asked me how to pray and whether I really think that prayer makes a difference. Others wondered why I would call these offerings "prayers" when none of them are addressed to a proper deity or reflective of a specific religious tradition. Some suggested calling them "blessings," "reflections," or "meditations" (all of which are beautiful words and none of which I object to using), and the back-and-forth continually challenged me to interrogate what I thought I was doing, why I was doing it, and for whom I was doing it.

I maintain the position that calling these offerings "prayers" does at least two things: It reclaims a word that has been weaponized and weakened and hopefully injects it with some revitalized energy, and it invites seekers to think of prayer as spiritual intentionality that can engender embodied action and change. In a world where fundamentalism has staked so much claim on the word "prayer," using a word like "blessing," "reflection," or "meditation" might seem a safer, less divisive bet, but why not use the more combustible word and welcome the conversation? How might prayer be reclaimed by a society that often dismisses magical thinking but is still in desperate need of awe, wonder, justice, and miracles? What if prayer were not a lazy cop-out from active engagement but the intentional invitation to active engagement? What if we prayed not only out of occasional helplessness and hopelessness but also to regularly open ourselves up to becoming the help, the hope, the justice, the miracles we need? What would happen if we met the overwhelming information cluttering our screens and our minds with prayerful intentionality every day? What if prayer is the simple and regular act of admitting our own individual vulnerability while remaining communally accountable to the most vulnerable among us? These questions have become increasingly important to me, not only in relationship to this continuing time of pandemic, but far beyond. What do we think we are doing when we pause, quietly focus ourselves, breathe, compose words, and attempt to connect to something larger than ourselves? What is prayer really *for*? I find that my beliefs best line up with the oft-quoted words from Søren Kierkegaard: "The function of prayer is not to influence God, but rather to change the nature of the one who prays."

The daily practice of writing these 366 prayers has changed me. Waking each morning, checking the news and checking in with my own mind and body, then choosing what prayer to put out into the universe have shaped the person I have become during this time. I have felt my attention and intention grow, even in a time when isolation, fear, and grief have threatened to overwhelm. I have felt my connection to the interdependence of us all grow. I have even been challenged to write prayers that scared me and trust that, by breathing these prayers out into the ether, some new breath might come back to me. Engaging with those who have read the prayers has offered life-giving buoys and connecting threads. Strangely, a solitary morning practice became a communal one as well, connecting me with people in ways I wouldn't have predicted during such a physically distant time.

The arc of these prayers openly reveals what was going on inside my own head and heart at the time they were composed. They were written rawly, often within the span of a few minutes. Depending on that day's news or a request from a reader or my own gut feeling, the prayers would tumble out. Sometimes specificity was called for; sometimes universality was the aim. As others engaged, some of the prayers would evolve into new versions of themselves. None of them were set in stone, and, even now, I don't consider any of them concretized. I believe that the act of praying (even for prayers that have been written down) must remain organic, dynamic, and open to adjustment, if it is to truly keep moving the soul. This collection might sometimes seem motley, but then, so were many of the year's events. Some of the prayers are praise songs; some are laments. More celebrity and hero deaths from COVID-19 necessitated celebrations of lives well lived. As racial-justice uprisings began with new passion following the police murder of George Floyd, the prayers took on a new dimension, incorporating a desire to support the protesters and organizers, all while attempting to stay connected to the virus threatening us all. More police murders of Black people called for recognition of lives stolen by systemic racism and the lies of white supremacy. As the United States geared up for a particularly contentious presidential election, the prayers became rallying cries for democracy and dismantling. Tense political races and terrifying climate events found their way into the mix, along with holidays and the passing of seasons.

And throughout the recollection of all these collective sea changes, certain prayers remind me of exactly where I was, emotionally, spiritually, sometimes physically, on certain days. I was diagnosed with COVID-19 myself on Christmas Eve 2020, and the prayers composed around that time were clearly the prayers that I needed to hear myself. As the vaccines began to roll out, the prayers filled with hope for their effectiveness and hope that they would make their way to the most marginalized among us. Toward the end of the collection, as we passed the one-year anniversary of the World Health Organization's declaring COVID-19 a global pandemic, I began to feel my own energy flagging. I now know that I was suffering from what has come to be known as "Long COVID," and some of the prayers from that time are obviously responses to my own aching body, heart, and mind. In that moment, as I realized that I was about to celebrate an entire year of writing these daily prayers and as I realized that I might not be able to keep it up, I also realized that it can be a spiritual practice in and of itself to know when it is time to let a practice go. I still pray daily, but my body told me it was the right moment to bring this public practice to a close. In a time when I have felt more in touch with my body's needs than ever, I have learned to listen more carefully to its wisdom. This is a good and necessary change to my own routine and one that I imagine many of us have experienced in new ways since COVID-19 came into our lives.

Change can come only through looking back candidly at where we've been, looking squarely at who we are, and looking forward to who we can become. The act of praying does this for me, and writing these "Tiny Prayers" has especially done this for me. Prayer doesn't have to be complicated, and it doesn't have to stay attached to the baggage that so many of us carry from damaging relationships with the invented, oppressive obsessions of organized religion. Prayer can be reclaimed as an everyday engagement with the real.

I purposely chose not to address any of these prayers to a "God" but rather to people, to places, to things, in an attempt to infuse the everyday with spiritual, mystical value. Every encounter we have in our daily lives, everything we read about in our newsfeeds, every everyday example of interdependence, of inspiration, even of evil, can be reframed as a sign of the times in which we live and a sign pointing us toward potential futures. These signs are all around us, even in the best of times, and they demand continuing participation, sincere contemplation, and constant transformation. Even as the acute threat of one plague ends, our world remains vulnerable to other plagues that need our attention and intention. It is my belief that these plagues (the continuing lies and violence of racism, classism, ableism, misogyny, homophobia, transphobia, white supremacy, Christian supremacy, colonialism, speciesism, extractivism, predatory capitalism, and their countless other insidious siblings) are spiritual issues that need spiritual alternatives.

And that is what prayer can offer. The only necessary ingredients for prayer are attention, intention, time, and quiet. This isn't a revelatory statement, but in a world more laden with distraction, apathy, productivity, and noise, it is radical. The more openly, honestly, and regularly we stop to articulate our reality, appreciate our interdependence, and acknowledge the issues affecting and connecting us all, the more agilely we can work together to consciously co-create new paths to collective liberation. Prayer invites us to interrogate and unlearn our most harmful lies and systems. Prayer re-orients us in disorienting times. Prayer requires and inspires commitment. The "Plague Year" during which these prayers were composed sometimes shows us at our worst, but it also shows us at our best, refusing to look away from the horrors in front of us and also refusing to let the horrors have the final say. When we pray together, we have the opportunity to point to the pain or to the pleasure, to name it and claim it, to ask ourselves, "OK, what now?" and to commit to answering that question. We can reframe the complicated to be an opportunity for creation. We don't need theology degrees to do it. We just need the will and one another.

I will be honored if you read this collection as an authentic account of many of the experiences that we collectively and individually encountered over the course of this "Plague Year," but I will be even more honored if you use these prayers as models for your own prayers, as guides for how you can approach every challenge, tragedy, joy, celebration, and beyond, in terrible years and in wonderful years, with attention and intention that will center you, offer you breath and pause, and send you back out into the world to do the co-creative, justice-seeking, spirit-fueled work that we are all called to name and pursue together.

Each of these "Tiny Prayers" concludes with the word "Amen," a word that has become so common that it's often casually treated as the end of something. But I like to think of the word "Amen" as more of an invitation, an articulation of an active spiritual imperative, a launchpad for a new beginning, a prodding to remind us to keep our promises to ourselves and to one another. Prayer evaporates if it stays stagnant on the page or hoarded in our hearts. It must be shared if it is to become more than words and nudge us to become more than we've been. I pray that you take these "Tiny Prayers" and the 366 "Amens" therein and find new beginnings. And, like all prayers, this collection is far from complete. It needs you. Luckily, just like our continuing collective work, this book doesn't end if you add your own prayers to it.

Amen.

The Book of Tiny Prayer

March 24, 2020

For Terrence McNally, playwright and librettist, who died of coronavirus complications

Thank you for giving unapologetically vibrant voice to queer love that will live forever, outlasting viruses that might kill bodies, but never Truth.

Amen

March 25, 2020

For healthcare workers

May you have enough moments of breath, enough moments of rest, enough voices saying, "You've got this," enough moments of simple calm in the midst of this storm, as you fight so lovingly to make sure we all have the same.

Amen

March 26, 2020

For faith leaders

May you remember that many of us don't
so much need to be brought back to a
rock-solid, fail-safe faith but rather invited
into an authentic conversation about fear,
mystery, and death, in order to find new
ways to live.

Amen

March 27, 2020

For those who are afraid

May you use the fears that keep you alert to
caring for yourself and others, reshape the
fears that nudge you toward new ways of
knowing yourself and others, and dismiss
the fears that lie and tell you neither is
possible.

Amen

March 28, 2020

For artists

May the spark of inspiration that so
thrilled you last night, then seemed
completely trite this morning, let you rest
for a bit, then bubble back up through
your imagination, messy with new energy,
begging to be explored as only you can.

Amen

March 29, 2020

For our bodies

May you do exactly what you are meant to
do, giving us information, telling us where
the pain is, moving to rhythms of heart
and lung, calling our attention not only to
parts in need, but also to all parts working
beautifully together.

Amen

March 30, 2020

For elected officials

May you care more about humans than attention, more about lives than markets; may you admit what you don't know and own up to what you do know, and may you remember that current reality must be faced in order to truly shape a future.

Amen

March 31, 2020

For Lorena Borjas, transgender- and immigrant-rights activist, who died of coronavirus complications

Thank you for embodying true motherhood as a daily mix of transforming pain into passion, reorganizing in the face of organized oppression, demanding community-building over wall-building, teaching those with power to use it well, and empowering those who fear they have none.

Amen

April 1, 2020

For our breath

May you stay steady, but may you also
offer gasps of wonder at how renewable
a resource you are, the only free gift
we continually pour into and take from
the world, each exhale announcing our
recommitment to every other living thing.

Amen

April 2, 2020

For striking workers

May your voices carry for those who have
no voice and for those whose lives need to
be interrupted, not only by fears of a virus,
but also by the cries of the human lives and
dreams that so often invisibly sustain our
decadence.

Amen

April 3, 2020

For Ellis Marsalis Jr., jazz musician and educator, who died of coronavirus complications

Thank you for teaching us that we can break rules and still be disciplined in our collaborative generosity, and that we can listen for the unique logic in even the music that doesn't immediately satisfy our own expectations.

Amen

April 4, 2020

For those who are grieving

May you seek solidarity and solitude as each is needed, may you feel empathy surround you, even when alone, and may you reject any calls to move through this more quickly, especially when they come from your own heart.

Amen

April 5, 2020

For those who are angry

May you remember that rage can be a step toward collective recommitment, inviting us to sustain steady flames together as we fight for change instead of burning out in a moment of individual combustion.

Amen

April 6, 2020

For those who are experiencing cabin fever

May you find solace in the fact that so many of us are also seeking surprises in too-familiar spaces, flashes of wonder in corners we know too well, moments of delight in too-similar days, and may this uncomfortable comfort connect us all.

Amen

April 7, 2020

For those who are detained

May you sense solidarity seeping through cracks in your prison walls, even as those of us outside taste only a small bit of your fear, your isolation, and your vulnerability, and may you know that many of us are fighting for all of us to be free.

Amen

April 8, 2020

For John Prine, singer-songwriter, who died of coronavirus complications

Thank you for telling us honest stories of ourselves, set to sweet melodies that allow them to sneak into our hearts, comforting us with universality, teasing our follies just enough to invite us to take ourselves a tad less seriously.

Amen

April 9, 2020

For those who are ill

May you reach out to those who will not
only comfort you but also help you to
secure the expert care you need, and may
you not be embarrassed to weep, rage, fear,
and be human, even as you trust this care
to both hold and heal you.

Amen

April 10, 2020

For essential workers

May you feel our deep gratitude, though
our smiles are hidden beneath our masks,
though our greetings come from several
feet away, and though, when we've been
told that we're safest inside, each day
beckons you back outside.

Amen

April 11, 2020

For those who are navigating their mental health

May you be kind to yourself,
acknowledging the weight that this current
fear adds to your plate, trusting the power
of your past resilience, even when it's
currently out of sight, and reaching out
to those who will simply accompany you
while not trying to fix anything.

Amen

April 12, 2020

For those who are far from those they love

May you have ample bandwidth, both for
your technological devices and for your
heart, and may you offer gratitude for the
ways we have to connect, even when apart,
but may you also be unafraid to call this
distance what it is: absolutely painful.

Amen

April 13, 2020

For David Driskell, artist, scholar, and curator, who died from coronavirus complications

Thank you for making an art of showcasing the overlooked, for using your own reality to draw attention to ignored realities, for gifting us with images both beautiful and troubling, inviting us to reflect on how our systems and lives are always both at the same time, and how only through creative interrogation can we own up to who we are and artfully evolve into who we say we want to be.

Amen

April 14, 2020

For postal workers

May you be assured to your core that, no matter what shallow messages you are receiving from our federal government, your lives, your employment, and the daily risks you are taking to keep our country connected matter deeply to us.

Amen

April 15, 2020

For those who are feeling stagnant

May you remember that your body and life are not mere tools for productivity (no matter what capitalism tells you) but rather dynamic, breathing realities that need rest, quiet, time, and space, and will organically tell you when they are ready to do and not just be again.

Amen

April 16, 2020

For those who are facing unemployment

May you feel surrounded by empathy, knowing that so many of us have been and are in the place where you are now, frightened, angry, seeking new paths, and may you find supporters who will both root

for your bright future and simply hold you
through this terrible present moment.

Amen

April 17, 2020

For farm workers

May you feel gratitude spreading and
surrounding you as more and more of us
become aware of how essential you are,
not because you put food on our table, but
because you are human beings, both strong
and vulnerable, who deserve and demand
ample government protections and ample
respect.

Amen

April 18, 2020

For our masks

May you protect our noses, our mouths,
our lungs, our lives, creating a system
whereby we all work together, precautions
not only for ourselves but also for others,
and may wearing you remind us that we

can still practice this communal care and cooperation even after the masks come off.

Amen

April 19, 2020

For those outside the epicenter

May you hear the pleas of those of us who are in the thick of it, and may you understand our urging you to stay home not as an attack on your perceived current freedoms but as a deep recommitment to a more just, more safe, more interconnected future freedom for all.

Amen

April 20, 2020

For those who are feeling just fine

May you enjoy this moment as a time when you can pour energy into this gift economy we sustain together, holding others through their lows, not forcing them to feel more fine than they are, trusting that there will be energy in the pool for you when you are feeling far less than fine.

Amen

April 21, 2020

For immigrants

May you rage against the inflaming racist, xenophobic, fascist overreaches by our federal government, and may you also feel the fiery fight continuing to spread in this country, with growing numbers of eager neighbors ready not only to welcome you, but also to enthusiastically celebrate you.

Amen

April 22, 2020

For the Earth

May you rest and breathe while so many of us abide indoors, may your plants grow freely, may your nonhuman animals sing and stretch wildly, may your clouded air clear, may your wounded lands heal, may your waters churn happily, and may we be so wowed by your beauty upon our reentrance that we finally get our act together and heed your warnings.

Amen

April 23, 2020

For parents and teachers

May you be filled with patience for yourself, appreciating the fact that what you are doing (engaging and educating our youngest in a time when they and you are frightened, distracted, and frustrated) is a monumental task with so few immediate rewards and so much immediate stress.

Amen

April 24, 2020

For our elders

May you feel enveloped in love, care, and respect, even if you cannot visit with your friends and family, even if the technology connecting so many of us feels alien and annoying, even if you fear that your winter years will be spent in deepening isolation, and may you deeply know how much we miss hugging you.

Amen

April 25, 2020

For those who currently have no shelter in which to shelter-in-place

May you encounter kindnesses on every corner, may you be offered not only funds but also guidance toward sustenance both edible and spiritual, may you be safe when you do find a place to rest, and may you be assured that many of us are fighting to end this housing crisis, even in the midst of this health crisis.

Amen

April 26, 2020

For those who are losing hope

May you find solace in the simple fact that uncertainty is not the opposite of hope but rather a natural and necessary aspect

of hope that keeps us on our toes and off
our high horses, and may you be assured
that unshakable surety is never required
in order for us to wake up, get out of bed,
get ready, and seek wonder, even in a world
that often feels far from wonderful.

Amen

April 27, 2020

For journalists

May you continue to ignore the attacks and
uncover the truth, always serving the good
of the people over the egos of the powerful,
and may you be assured that your integrity
is always quietly appreciated, even as the
loudest, most vitriolic voices continue to
blather in your direction.

Amen

April 28, 2020

For Dr. Lorna M. Breen, medical director of the Emergency Department at New York–Presbyterian Allen Hospital

Thank you for your tireless service, for your compassionate leadership, for your open heart, for embodying the role of "Hero" without ever seeking the title of "Hero," for your remarkable life, which will continue to be a remembered blessing coursing through every breath of every life you have touched, healed, and saved.

Amen

April 29, 2020

For those who are feeling "meh"

May you settle into this gray, liminal space, this place somewhere between panic and ease, between despair and faith, between down and up, may you feel the strange sense of balance that comes from being honest about the just-okay, the just-enough, the just-getting-by, and may you

trust that this is a perfectly–imperfectly
valid spot for you to exist for a while.

Amen

April 30, 2020

For sanctuary cities

May you hold fast to your spiritual
imperative to protect and empower,
may you continue to be models for cities
everywhere, and as a racist, fascist,
nationalistic empire threatens our states
with bogus, illegal, and unnecessary
deals, and falsely claims that we must
choose between heart and health, may you
continue to declare loudly that we can and
must always have both.

Amen

May 1, 2020

For those who are finding it difficult to focus

May you take a moment to make a list of
your current tasks ("current" meaning

immediate, not days or weeks from now)
in order of priority, not so you get all of
them done today, and not even so you get
any of them done today, but simply because
making a map of the landscape in front of
you not only might make the terrain a tad
less treacherous but might even make the
trail a tad more inviting.

Amen

May 2, 2020

For Black communities

May you hold this country accountable, not
only to history but to the continued ways
in which our current moment exposes this
country's rampant, unchecked, systemic
racism, be that in the form of armed white
people encouraged by our administration
to threaten us all or in the form of this
virus affecting Black bodies in far larger
ways, spotlighting the blatantly intentional
failings of our infrastructure, and may all
of us with privilege admit that we must
transcend today's harm and half-hearted

gestures if we truly wish to transform tomorrow.

Amen

May 3, 2020

For the youngest among us

May you observe this time with deep curiosity, recognizing the suffering of a society that has not grown up even as its consumption and production have grown, and as you yourself mature, may you continually choose to contribute to a collective growing-up, paying close, careful attention, especially after we're told we can return to blissfully bankrupt ignorance.

Amen

May 4, 2020

For those who are feeling more drained than usual

May you remember that your body is completely confused, with your limbs far less active during waking hours and your

brain working overtime, with all parts
anxiously keeping a score of your fears,
your disappointments, and your stress even
when unconscious, and may you be gentle
with yourself and with one another as,
right now, we're also all parts of one big,
confused, tired, collective body.

Amen

May 5, 2020

For those who don't want things to return to "normal"

May you continue to connect to the
growing number of people who are
responding to this tragic moment by
reimagining organizing, activism, and
mutual aid, refusing to allow the status
quo to sweep back in too quickly and
dangerously, as we find new ways to
care for communal need, hear the call of
a picture bigger than individual wants,
and learn to be something far more
thoughtfully dynamic than "normal."

Amen

May 6, 2020

For transit workers

May you continue to loudly shed light on
the hurried, unhealthy conditions that
our society so often allows to stay buried
underground or bottled up in buses, until
we can move ourselves to more carefully
celebrate and protect the human beings
who regularly risk their own lives to keep
city life bright and bustling.

Amen

May 7, 2020

For those in states that are reopening

May you be enveloped in safety, and when
you know in your heart that your leaders
and fellow citizens aren't aiding in that,
may you have the strength and means
to envelop yourself in safety, finding
ways to steer clear of crowds, to model
mask-wearing, and to spread wisdom
in a country that can't seem to wrap its
collective brain around the simple facts
that lives are always more important than

money and that boredom should never be
the basis of any decision.

Amen

May 8, 2020

For those who are feeling lonely

May you give yourself ample time to
discover new ways to hold yourself, new
ways to appreciate what good company
you are for yourself, new ways to reshape
monotony into moments of quiet,
affectionate self-reflection, and when those
ways do fail (and they do sometimes), may
you have the self-assurance to reach out to
another, someone who will probably say,
"Oh, thanks for reaching out! I was getting
a little lonely."

Amen

May 9, 2020

For New York City

May we continue to hum with the energy
of who we really are beneath all of this,

a city of friendly strangers, unabashedly
bumping against one another, rushed and
filled with the rush of possibility, loud
with laughter and protest, packed with
creativity and diversity, even as our streets
lie in quiet wait, and may we use this time
to examine ourselves, our systems, our
failures and fantasies, so that when we
wake up in this city that so rarely sleeps,
we will stay awake to the call of who we
really can be.

Amen

May 10, 2020

For those who mother in myriad ways

May you feel the love and nurture you
pour into the world come flooding back
to you in waves of gratitude, of patience,
of commitment to interdependence, and
may we all remember that the power of
mothering is most profoundly felt in subtle,
simple nudges, like reminders to take care
of one another, to listen, to ask for what we

need, to admit to our mistakes, to try again, and to wash our hands.

Amen

May 11, 2020

For those who are losing patience

May you seek ways to trade in that growing feeling of irritability for a deeper sense of humor, not because any of this is funny but because the gift of not taking oneself too seriously might just clear away the debilitating dread of unnecessarily critical self-focus and nurture the space, time, energy, and lightness we need to take our commitments to the rest of the world a bit more seriously.

Amen

May 12, 2020

For Dr. Anthony Fauci, immunologist and Director of the U.S. National Institute of Allergy and Infectious Diseases

May you feel gratitude surround you today as you hold firm to your own expert opinion, certain that you have done the work, knowing that you have already grieved the fact that you will be further maligned by many and have balanced that sorrow with the assurance that you will also continue to be the voice of radical reason for many more, and may your message of ultimately hopeful caution spread more quickly than this virus, changing hearts, minds, and the current course of human history.

Amen

May 13, 2020

For those who are tired of looking at screens

May you remember that, just as with
life outside your home, when your body,
brain, and eyes are weary, you can take
a break from the glare, the stress, the
relentless push to be connected, you can
say, "No, thank you," to invitations, you
can limit a typically hour-long meeting
to thirty minutes, you can be honest with
yourself and with one another about the
fact that having tools to communicate can
simultaneously be mightily amazing and
mightily tiresome, and you can power
down, reschedule, and pick it all back up
another day.

Amen

May 14, 2020

For the Navajo Nation

May your cries for investment in
infrastructure that values your relationship
with the natural world be heard, absorbed,

and heeded, acknowledging the colonizing
trail of broken promises, stolen land,
and brutal violence that has blazed for
centuries, long before this pandemic shed
new light on the build-up of intentional
failings that now allows this virus to ravage
your land and bodies, and may all of us
with privilege gain enough insight to fight
for and with you, not only to heal this
immediate pain but also to listen to the
open, ages-old wounds that will remain.

Amen

May 15, 2020

For the CDC

May you hold firm to your mission to
offer life-saving, expert, and detailed
guidelines, despite the greed of those who
cannot bring themselves to honor people
over profit, and may you be lifted by the
abundant gratitude and solidarity beaming
at you from so many of us, shedding stark
light on the rampant spread of shadowy,
money-obsessed misinformation.

Amen

May 16, 2020

For those who are graduating remotely

May you feel the same rush you would
were you traveling triumphantly across a
stage, diploma in hand, an effervescent mix
of accomplishment, fear, and dreamy vision
beating loudly in your heart, and may you
be honest about the fact that the absence of
pomp and tradition is a true bummer, but
may you still know that you have achieved
something remarkable today, that you have
overcome remarkable obstacles to get here,
and that, even via the virtual, we all await,
in vibrantly real life, the remarkable ways
in which your vision will change a world
sorely in need of you.

Amen

May 17, 2020

For those who refuse to wear a mask

May you be engulfed in wisdom and
empathy, surprising yourself with how
freeing it feels to connect your own life to

the lives of those around you, and may you admit to yourself that a little individual discomfort, a little extra individual effort, is really nothing compared with the enormity of both continued danger and potential safety for all.

Amen

May 18, 2020

For those who are keeping watch on the data

May you absorb the voices of experts warning that what we know now reflects only what was happening weeks ago, making this information frustratingly out of date by the time it arrives, and may you continue to accept this truth humbly, no matter how bored you are, realizing that, although this reality remains very complicated, the individual response required remains very simple: Stay home, or if you cannot, cover your face and keep your distance.

Amen

May 19, 2020

For those who are feeling down and don't know why

May you take a long pause and a deep
breath, may you stop thinking that you
need to explain this inexplicable feeling to
anyone, even yourself, may you remember
that this place is not a permanent
residence, that you have been here before
and will leave again, return again, and leave
again, and may the reminder that you know
this daily balancing act well bring you a bit
of inexplicable balance today.

Amen

May 20, 2020

For those in states that are opening more slowly

May you appreciate this cautious approach,
even with its continued inconveniences,
even with its economic uncertainty, even
with its frustrations and fears, and may you
spend a moment today offering gratitude
for this kind of slowness we are getting to

know, this kind of slowness that protects and calms and pays attention, which is quite different from the power-hoarding hang-ups that truly delay justice, the kind of slowness this country often knows too well.

Amen

May 21, 2020

For those who want to scream

May you let it out, really, at full volume, for as long as you need and as often as you need, trusting that anyone who hears will know exactly why you're doing it and perhaps even give themselves allowance to do the same, simply because they witnessed the sound of your full-throated authenticity.

Amen

May 22, 2020

For our future

May you invite us to be creators, seekers, and listeners, not merely clumsy predictors, and may you remind us that humbly and thoughtfully transforming into who we need to be, for ourselves and for one another, is far less daunting and far more achievable than magically thinking that we can foresee some predestined, perfect other side to all of this.

Amen

May 23, 2020

For congregations of faith

May you trust that the most essential spiritual imperative you hold is to nurture health; may you remember that you need not be inside your buildings for you to pray, connect, sing, dance, rejoice, and do basically everything you need to do; and may you keep your physical spaces closed

so you may continue to keep your spiritual
lives open and thriving.

Amen

May 24, 2020

For those we've lost

May your lives be remembered for the
unique gifts they were and remain to this
world, may those who mourn your deaths
find some comfort in those memories, and
may all of us view these memories as clear
and continuing calls to recommit to saving
as many lives and memories as possible.

Amen

May 25, 2020

For those who don't feel brave

May you appreciate the fact that bravery
comes most often in the form of a steady
sustaining of integrity and character, and
may you trust that today basically calls you
to be willing to find simple and attainable
ways to sustain your own life while

sustaining the lives of others, tasks for
which you are more than ready and able.

Amen

May 26, 2020

For those who can't remember what day it is

May you find solace in the fact that so
many of us are in this same time-smearing
boat, weeks and weekends blending
together, some hours flying by and others
seemingly endless, and may we all realize
that these structures we've imposed on
our lives are built for a reality we are not
currently experiencing, grant grace to
ourselves and to one another, look at the
calendar, and calmly carry on.

Amen

May 27, 2020

For those who just can't deal with this country anymore

May your raging heartache meet the
raging heartache of so many of us,
diverse in degrees of privilege but united
in the shared horror that true honesty,
justice, and equity still elude this society,
racism infecting our shared body just as
deeply as any virus, and may this aching
rage grow, through loud education and
self-interrogation, until we actively
acknowledge that this body will not truly
be well until all can breathe, live, and
thrive freely.

Amen

May 28, 2020

For Larry Kramer, writer and activist

Thank you for your loudness, for your
relentlessness, for your crankiness,
for your overwhelmingly committed,
imperfect, undying love for all of us, and
for your comfort zone–demolishing refusal

to allow our own complacency to ever
silence our duty to act up in the face of the
truly unacceptable.

Amen

May 29, 2020

For those who are protesting

May your cries dig painfully into each
of our hearts until we are all dragged
out of our own quiet, and may your act
of doing something generative with
your rage compel us all to do something
generative with our rage, always listening
most deeply to those most suffocated by
violent, systematized oppression, and
showing up in every way possible, through
amplification, education, association, and
donations.

Amen

May 30, 2020

For bus drivers who are refusing to transport protesters to precincts

May your modeling of unmovable solidarity move us all, may we all witness the powerful potential of refusing to offer our services and loyalties to the very power structures that rampantly run over the most powerless, and may this country, at long last, do the work we must do in order to choose a different destination.

Amen

May 31, 2020

For those who feel or are unable to protest in the streets

May you remember that there are many ways to contribute to a movement, that this pandemic has taught us that we can connect, support, and make change even when we can't be in the physical spaces we wish to be inhabiting, and that all of us are needed, no matter where we are, because this is a deep dismantling of centuries of oppression, requiring a commitment that must last far longer than any temporary moment of quarantine.

Amen

June 1, 2020

For injured protesters

May your wounds heal and your bodies rest, may you feel the solidarity and gratitude of so many surrounding you as you restore yourself to fight again, may this country open its collective heart to see the true root of the violence, the true source of the stress, the festering sores that white supremacist power continually salts, and may we bear witness to these injuries, naming them loudly before we rush to cover them with our same old tired, ineffectual Band-Aids.

Amen

June 2, 2020

For queer folks

May you center your pride in the truth
that the foundation of our community's
liberation was birthed by the fed-up
strength of trans women of color, may that
centering demand that we each come out,
again and again, against white supremacy
and colonization, against state-sanctioned
brutality, against our own tendencies to
assimilate and co-opt, and may we all
continue to fly our mutual aid freak flags
long past any government-issued curfew
and long past June.

Amen

June 3, 2020

For those who are glued to their screens and/or the streets

May you make plans to regularly step away
for several moments a day, knowing that
the news is out there, that the fight is out
there, that the sustaining of a movement is
bigger than you, that it requires you to take

care of your body and soul, which means
breathing into the horrors you already
know, taking a break from ingesting
more, and trusting your communities to
continually balance the work, staggering
participation so that the collective spirit
moves, even during the moments when you
are at necessary rest.

Amen

June 4, 2020

For George Perry Floyd Jr., killed by police in Minneapolis

Thank you for the loving life you lived and
for the leadership you modeled, truths
that will be celebrated as memorials
for your life begin today, and may these
memorials continue to underline the fact
that you were born to live, not simply to be
a hashtag, that you were born to breathe,
not simply to be a symbol, that the racist
systems of this country have stolen your
life and forced you into this hashtag-
symbol status, and that we must not simply
memorialize but do the work, until all

Black lives can live and breathe freely, and there are no more needs for hashtags or symbols.

Amen

June 5, 2020

For Breonna Taylor, killed by police in Louisville

Thank you for your spirit and service, for the help you brought to the world and the dedication you brought to that work, and on this, what would have been your twenty-seventh birthday, as we highlight and hashtag names, may we always remember your life, may we condemn the systemic, racist violence that ended it, may we demand accountability from those who stole it, and may we commit ourselves to never forgetting and loudly celebrating the contributions and courage of Black women, not only after their deaths, but also while they live and lead us.

Amen

June 6, 2020

For those who are listening

May you realize that this is just the next
step of a never-ending process, that this
will always be about continuing hygiene,
that these current reforms to public policy,
to cruel systems, to centuries of brutality,
are only the next wave of a necessary sea
change, and may you know that you can
weather this sea by continuing to listen,
continuing to act, continuing to swim here
in these uncomfortable waters, inviting
more and more people deeper in, especially
when the masses try to head back to the
comfortable shore too early.

Amen

June 7, 2020

For those who are feeling galvanized

May you take this shot of hopeful
adrenaline and, as you use most of it to
fuel your energetic participation in this
moment, may you also preserve some
of it in the deepest part of your heart,

remembering that this high will probably
also give way to moments of individual
and collective discouragement, and that
it is in those low moments that you will
need to go to your reserves, take that bit
of hope you've saved, remember that this
is a movement, not just a collection of
moments, refuel, and keep moving.

Amen

June 8, 2020

For the Minneapolis City Council, following their pledge to defund and dismantle the city's police department

May your active witness be a model for
all cities, calling each to realize how
powerfully simple a first step can be when
those with power listen to those with
imagination, may you stay firm to your
vote, especially as it is challenged by those
with no vision, and may your example
push us all to continue to broaden our
own imaginations, until the power of the
racist, historical status quo gives way to

a sweeping, creativity-fueled, prophetic reshaping of community support, sustenance, and safety for all.

Amen

June 9, 2020

For those who are waking up

May you trust this bright, shining feeling and share it eagerly with others, especially those who are still aching to get up and those who are actively rolling over and going back to sleep, and may you deeply appreciate that your most important imperative now is not to proudly hold your own healthily lit wick high and out of reach, but to offer it forward to light the wicks that are struggling to catch fire themselves.

Amen

June 10, 2020

For those who are uncomfortable

May you think back on each truly
transformative moment of your life and
remember that you were breathtakingly
uneasy every time, may you hold these
memories as the reactivating sustenance
you need now, especially whenever you
feel like quitting, going back into hiding, or
clinging to chains of comfort, and may you
listen closely to the pangs, appreciating
each as a very necessary step toward a new
kind of freedom, for all and for you.

Amen

June 11, 2020

For those who are afraid of messing up

May you take this fear and reshape it
into thoughtful, generous intention, not
worrying about getting anything perfect
but rather trusting a combination of your
gut and those around you to tell you when
you might listen instead of talk, when you

might welcome education and invitation, and when you might let go of your ego and simply say, "I'm sorry. Let me try that again."

Amen

June 12, 2020

For those who see change on the horizon

May you take in this vision and know that your next step is to move from witness to testifier, from admirer to co-creator, from absorber to enactor, a shift that requires a thoughtful balance of speaking up about things that matter, breathing through things that don't, questioning your own fragile assumptions, strengthening the muscles required to lift up the voices that challenge you, and actively becoming that change you see coming, instead of simply waiting for it to arrive.

Amen

June 13, 2020

For those who are overwhelmed by the enormity of the work ahead

May you tread this vast, deep whirlpool, feeling this movement buoyed by mutual aid, countless helpers lifting each task together, and if you are new to this fight, may you see what has been accomplished in just a matter of days, and if you have been fighting this fight for years, may you see the fruits of that commitment surging vibrantly to life, calling more and more souls to this communally supported churning, each gift of individual generosity pouring sustainability into these expanding waves of collaborative motion.

Amen

June 14, 2020

For trans, gender noncomforming, and nonbinary folks

May you deeply know that you are nothing less than our brightest hopes for the future, and as the government challenges your rights, as celebrities malign your identities, as society both exoticizes and harms your bodies, as the mainstream media quickly move past your stories and struggles, may you also deeply know that a growing chorus of us are committed to speaking up, calling out, and fighting like heaven to make sure that you are not only our brilliant future but also seen, valued, celebrated, and protected now, here, in our slowly but steadily queering present.

Amen

June 15, 2020

For those who are entering difficult conversations

May you remember that authenticity is not an attack, that perfection is not the point, that creating relationships is a constantly evolving act, and may you offer yourself wholly, listening for the pain inside what's actually being said, feeling yourself not merely leaving your old assumptions behind but actively, carefully co-creating something packed with honest-to-goodness possibility.

Amen

June 16, 2020

For the Supreme Court of the United States, following its *Bostock* decision, holding that the 1964 Civil Rights Act protects gay, lesbian, and transgender employees from discrimination

May you feel the cries of celebration beaming your way today, not because you have handed us a gift but because you have listened to collective wisdom and collective heart and combined both with your collective power to make change, and may you remember that you can always do this with every decision you make, and that we will absolutely be here to applaud you when you do and to challenge you when you need a reminder to pay attention to the more fabulous angels of your nature.

Amen

June 17, 2020

For those who are still afraid to come out

May you be lifted by the progress and
protections shifting all around you, and
may you find the support you need to
sustain this lift, recognizing that this
kind of encouragement doesn't always
come from biological family, and knowing
that, even with progress and protections,
dangers still lurk, and may you find clear
pathways to chosen family unfolding,
beckoning you to leave the isolating harm
of the closet and to move confidently
into the open air, trusting that there are
countless others who know this journey
well and who will lovingly travel right
alongside you, following your own unique
pace.

Amen

June 18, 2020

For those who are having to change their minds

May you generously examine evidence that is new to you, may you call yourself to continually witness the lived experiences of the oppressed, especially when they challenge the core givens you've always taken for granted, may you normalize the act of humble question-asking and honest self-interrogation, and may you never stop becoming a better version of yourself.

Amen

June 19, 2020

For a country confronting its history

May you stay forever passionate about this dismantling, long after the news cycle stops covering it, long after the trend-followers move on to other things, long after you have exited your comfort zone and entered a new life of transformative discomfort, and may you always remember that, once the spotlight shifts away, it is in the daily drudgery of the personal and the political that the deepest, realest work continues.

Amen

June 20, 2020

For residents of the Greenwood district, site of the 1921 Tulsa race massacre

May you be surrounded by safety and solidarity as you continue your Juneteenth festivities while blatant racism and danger gather right outside your community's perimeter, and may the memory of the horrors that happened there a century ago mix with the images of this current brazen act of white supremacist gathering and remind us all that this country has so far to go, that we cannot even begin to address scars if we keep exacerbating open wounds, and that reparations must be actively offered in order for repair to be even remotely possible.

Amen

June 21, 2020

For those who father in myriad ways

May you continue to seek pathways to
parenting that extend beyond the merely
biological or patriarchal, embodying the
fact that each of us is an ever-evolving
combination of child and parent, gathering
collective wisdom to pass down to the
next generation and collective gratitude to
pass up to those who have taught us how
to grow, and may we all always seek and
model mutuality over muscle, solidarity
over stoicism, and co-creative community
over cruel callousness.

Amen

June 22, 2020

For a city entering a new phase

May you stay alert to the threat of an
oncoming wave of new illness, but may
you also remember that this wave is simply
a new part of an ongoing threat, one that
you have been and remain fully equipped
to weather by covering your face, washing

your hands, keeping your distance, and
protecting your spirit, and may you not
allow yourself to be daunted by fear of
drowning, knowing that, no matter how
large a wave it is, you have the knowledge,
tools, and skills required to stay afloat.

Amen

June 23, 2020

For the bubbles on our ballots

May you be so filled with the ink of our
pens that the hope we pour into you
spills over, flowing out past the walls of
our "privacy booths," connecting every
heart, every hand, every vote, and may
you become bubbles that do much more
than register data, floating high enough to
surprise, clinging one to another, modeling
how to dance a revolution, admitting fear
of fragility, opening wider and wider,
encircling us in bigger shapes, beyond
what myopic human imaginations can
conjure, reminding us that there is an "us"

bubbling somewhere beneath it all, even, and especially, when we are partitioned off.

Amen

For those who are still following the public safety rules

May the simple gift of your thoughtful wisdom tendril out and model unselfish humanity for all, and may everyone you encounter internalize how easy and necessary it is to de-center one's own immediate comfort, re-center one's own public promise to their neighbors, and re-enter a daily practice of visible, replicable, communal recommitment to sustaining the bare minimum: life and health for all.

Amen

June 25, 2020

For those who just don't know where to start

May you take a step toward humility today,
seeking education, making a connection,
asking a question, investigating a privilege,
a bias, a given, an assumption, and may
you be honest with yourself about the
daunting reality of how much work there
is to do, but may you also be honest with
others about your need for collaboration,
knowing that this work is not yours to do
alone, and also knowing that this fact does
not clear you of individual obligation but
rather demands your daily, active, evolving
participation in the continuing co-creative
work.

Amen

June 26, 2020

For those who are occupying New York City Hall, demanding cuts to the NYPD budget

May your bodies be surrounded by safety and your spirits surrounded by solidarity, may your voices and demands be heard by those with the power to enact sweeping change, and may your prophetic witness teach us all to light fresh pathways to equity beyond our easy status quos, economic justice beyond our boring quick fixes, and reparative visions beyond our wildest human imaginings.

Amen

June 27, 2020

For those who are holding too much inside

May you remember that this near-bursting feeling is the steady growth of your empathy muscle, keeping you alive, keeping you transforming, keeping you committed to all other living beings, and

when this seems overwhelming, when
the pressure threatens to crack your own
structure, may you remember that our
individual task is never to seek to contain it
on our own, but to open up and out, fusing
with the tendons, muscles, and bones of
everyone around us, until we together
create larger, sturdier, more flexible
systems to share the weight.

Amen

June 28, 2020

For the forequeers who have gotten us this far

May you feel enveloped in gratitude
today as we proudly honor the largest
and smallest steps toward liberation, may
you feel how deeply your fierce, scarred
spirits move with and through us, may
your voices join ours as we cry out that
liberation is not complete until all can
taste it, hold it, and share it, and may you
bask in new possibility, as we take this
communal passion to the streets, mixing
our celebrations of progress with our

memories of pain and our demands for continuing change, marching forward, nudging, stretching, and carrying this world into far queerer, more liberative tomorrows.

Amen

June 29, 2020

For those who are having trouble speaking up

May you reframe your own discomfort as a new kind of freedom, a breaking of societal tethers that have taught you that keeping the peace is the key to your own survival, that complaining quietly is the way to remain politic, and may you push yourself to listen closely for what is actually being demanded of you in each moment, find every oppressive crack where the raising of your voice is necessary, and connect your activating unease to every struggle for liberation, especially those you could conveniently, silently ignore.

Amen

June 30, 2020

For those whose work–life boundaries are blurring

May you allow yourself more leeway
to be discombobulated, knowing that
discombobulation is currently the literal
state of the world, may you have respect
not only for the hours you have committed
to addressing the needs of others but
also for the hours you must commit to
attending to your own needs, and may you
clear through the confusing fog to find a
system that supports not just your desire to
do more but also your body's demand that
you find time to do less.

Amen

July 1, 2020

For those who just don't know how they're feeling

May you pause and stop trying to
name your mood, appreciating that
some completely defy categorization,
remembering that this is not the first time

that the emotional mix inside you has been
utterly unclassifiable and that you're still
here to tell those stories, may you listen to
yourself a bit more deeply today, hearing
all of the twisty nuances that make you
complicatedly, gloriously human, and may
you simply love everything you are.

Amen

July 2, 2020

For those who just can't understand how busy they feel

May you remember that there is an added
layer of stress and sadness to everything
you are doing right now, that we are all
confronting a maddening disconnect,
even in the midst of our most mundane
activities, that making daily decisions
about masks, sheltering, safety, health,
and an uncertain future is a full-time job
(on top of all of our other work!), may we
acknowledge that this added line to our
job description is actually impossible to do
well, because we've had no real training,
and may this knowledge fill us with

uncommon patience for one another, and
especially for ourselves.

Amen

For those who are discovering way too many new things about themselves

May you take these surprises, the attractive
and the less attractive, and acknowledge
that these fragments of your personality
and history have always existed inside you,
some flying more stealthily under your
own radar than others, and may you invite
yourself into a more intentional mode of
self-reflection, nurturing the surprises that
offer strength and healing and reshaping
the surprises that conjure fear and anxiety,
comforted by the fact that you are far
from alone in this present mirror-gazing,
that your individual self-excavation is
important to a collective reckoning, and
that your introspective discoveries are

vital to the sustaining of this continuing
communal revelation.

Amen

July 4, 2020

For those who simply can't celebrate this holiday

May you send solidarity to those who are
fighting for this country to own up to its
massive failures and live up to its own
promises, may you give gratitude to those
who have poured their passion into the
transformations that we now so often
take for granted, and may you challenge
yourself to continually exist in the sweet,
generous spot between independence and
interdependence, until collective freedom
is not just a hopeful destination but an
actively lived reality.

Amen

July 5, 2020

For those who are still reflecting on the change that needs to come

May you take this reflection and turn it into action, seeking continuing education, especially when it is inconvenient or overwhelming, learning that it is not enough to simply admire those who are rising up, speaking out, unearthing, and dismantling, but that admiration must always inspire motion if it is to be anything but empty, and that true creation is not a spectator sport but must rather become an ever-deepening, ever-spreading invitation to collaboration, especially for those who could easily continue to watch from the sidelines.

Amen

July 6, 2020

For those who were doing fine, then weren't, then were, and now maybe aren't again

May you continue to listen curiously to the irregular rhythms of your moods, not in an attempt to master the highs or avoid the lows but rather to become a more agile improvisor of your own melody, and may you allow the harmony and dissonance of those around you to give your own tune depth and assurance, because we're all making strange new noises and learning uncomfortable new songs lately, so we might as well make weird, fun, honest music together, and stop trying to do it all alone.

Amen

July 7, 2020

For those who just want a hug

May you reach out to someone today, through a screen or maybe just a shift of your eyes over the brim of your mask, and invent a new sign of affection, and for just a moment, instead of focusing on the current scarcity of our most common modes of physical contact, may you focus on the abundance of creativity this time requires, have fun with the challenge, and become an inventor of a new language, new customs, and newly deepened connection.

Amen

July 8, 2020

For those who see big transitions approaching

May you lean into this oncoming change with the eager excitement you reserve for real possibilities, may you trust that you have the smarts and the heart to create an art of adjustment, and when the steps get a bit trickier, may you stop trying to control every move, welcome fumbles and falls, and have a rousing good time becoming who, in your deepest parts, you already are.

Amen

July 9, 2020

For our educators

May you feel surrounded by gratitude for
the love and expertise you bring to your
vocation, and as our elected officials hem
and haw about money, politics, and power,
may you deeply know how appreciated
your work is, may you deeply know that
you are the keepers and sharers of wisdom,
of ethics, of history, all things we sorely
need right now, and may you deeply know
how many of us are prepared to fight with
you to make certain that deep education
overcomes shallow greed.

Amen

July 10, 2020

For those who are seeking asylum

May your continuing journey be moored
by the steadfast solidarity of so many of us,
and as we fight the latest proposed gutting
of this country's already cruel, dismissive,
racist laws, may you feel the fierce push of
activists and organizers, documented and

undocumented, as we lift up your stories
and lives, collectively bending the moral
arc of our history toward the embodied
welcome, safety, liberty, and justice that
this country has yet to truly, freely offer all.

Amen

July 11, 2020

For those who are feeling strangely upbeat

May you nurture this feeling and neither
hoard nor ignore its nudging, assured that
bursts of joy reveal a renewable resource
far deeper and more lasting than mere
happiness, and that glimmers of personal
peace do not deny the very real suffering
that plagues this world but rather fortify
a sustainable foundation to cradle our
constant pain, and may you be unafraid to
gently share this subtle power, not to force
inauthentic smiles on anyone but rather
to remind us all that there is something
beautiful blossoming beneath even those

muddier moments when harmony feels far harder to unearth.

Amen

For those who are finding it difficult to face the day

May you offer yourself ample patience, appreciating the fact that you know your body and mind better than anyone else does, and may you resolve to take three steps: get up, make your bed, and get dressed, knowing that, once these things are done, you will be three steps into the day, and may you then reach out to someone who will not nudge you to immediately go further but will simply wait with you until you know what next step you'd like to take.

Amen

July 13, 2020

For those who don't think they can pray

May you find a moment, perhaps right now, to stop where you are, to quiet yourself, to pause your hurried timeline, to settle into the present, to focus on your breath, and as you breathe in what the world has to offer you and breathe out what you have to offer the world, may you give gratitude for what you have, may you tend to the places where you ache, may you ask how you might commit to change, and may you then go back into your day knowing that you have prayed.

Amen

July 14, 2020

For those who feel the weight of the world on their shoulders

May you remember that the idea of pulling oneself up by one's bootstraps has always been a myth, that no one in the history of this planet has ever carried anything

completely by themselves, and that this
continuing heavy lifting is something
you should not, and actually cannot, do
by yourself, and may this knowledge fill
you with strange comfort and a desire to
reach out to those who exercise right by
your side, balancing this interdependent
carrying with you, even when you fear
you're on your own.

Amen

July 15, 2020

For those who can't find the right words

May you allow yourself time to process
your thoughts, to tend to your feelings, to
sit with yourself and with others, knowing
that many things, if not most, are beyond
language and can be explored only in
the silence between words, where deep
listening replaces our own desire to be
right or to articulate and draws us instead
into humble co-creation that we could
never achieve by ourselves.

Amen

July 16, 2020

For those who are burning the candle at both ends

May you halt this unsurprising but unsustainable habit, admitting that this feeling that you must do it all right now is an unfair demand that capitalism has cruelly drilled into your soul, may you listen to the aches in your body, the chaos in your brain, and the shortness in your breath, may you promise your heart, your mind, and your lungs that you will take an unproductive moment to rest, and may you surprise and delight yourself by actually keeping your promise.

Amen

July 17, 2020

For those who are feeling messy

May you open your heart to yourself, realizing that we rarely have enough patience for our own messiness, may you look around and see how we are all basically messy children pretending to be grown up, may you think of the person in your life who has shown you the most patient love, and may you patiently love yourself and your messiness as deeply as they have.

Amen

July 18, 2020

For John Lewis, congressman

Thank you for offering the fierce gifts of your mind, heart, and body on the front lines, for your unbeatable commitment to racial equity, for your dedication to teaching us how to march for freedom, to run for office, to use one's power to empower all, and as we mourn your death and celebrate your life, as your own marching and running end, may we embody your modeling of unstoppable justice-seeking and carry your spirit through the hard work that remains.

Amen

July 19, 2020

For those who are finding it difficult to be optimistic

May you welcome the nonbinary
knowledge that optimism and pessimism
are not your only choices, and may you
commit to a truth in between, a truth that
exists even when you don't remember
it, that you have resources, community,
and your own gifts to offer, that there is
meaning, even when the path ahead is
unclear, and may you stop trying to force
assured steps and instead wander with the
rest of us for a while.

Amen

July 20, 2020

For those whose hearts are hurting

May you pinpoint that painful place where
it feels like a vice is squeezing away your
life and joy, then may you feel for the
persistent pulse beneath that pain, may
you marvel at how your heart, even under
duress, is still beating out a rhythm for the

rest of your body to follow, and may you follow that rhythm, knowing that the pain will eventually transform into something else, and that this steady beat is always available, especially when you need to find your groove again.

Amen

July 21, 2020

For protesters in Portland, Oregon, following the deployment of the National Guard

May you feel solidarity pouring in from all sides, as you enact your constitutional rights, as you embody your spiritual calling to resist tyranny whenever it rears its head, as you face what could be in store for so many of our cities, and may safety surround you as you show us all how deeply necessary protest is, how deeply dangerous imperial power is, and how deeply hope-fueled this continuing fight must be.

Amen

July 22, 2020

For those who need to cry

May you give yourself generous permission
to simply let your tears fall, in private,
in public, trusting that every single
person around you also has tears closer
to brimming over than they might care
to admit, and may your act of allowance
extend to others, inviting all to think of
their need to weep not as a weakness,
but as proof of the honest ocean that is
constantly connecting us, even when we
try to dam its flow.

Amen

July 23, 2020

For those who are filled with fury

May you listen to this feeling, thanking
it for doing exactly what it's supposed to
be doing, keeping you alert and humming
with energy, and may you trouble this
emotion not only by focusing on what you
are against but also by focusing on what
you are for, what is keeping you going, who

is bringing you joy and hope, where you see
yourself contributing to change, and may
you not dismiss your anger but realize that
it is only the first step toward something
far more freeing.

Amen

July 24, 2020

For those who don't know their next step

May you accept this uncertainty and even
celebrate it, acknowledging how clearly
a lack of surety calls you into the present
moment, where you cannot predict the
future and must be honest about that fact,
where you are instead called to listen
deeply to your heart in ways that you
often skip, where possibilities abound, and
may you check in with yourself, may you
pay attention to your instincts, may you
question your assumptions, and then may
you make a boldly humble move.

Amen

July 25, 2020

For those who fear they've lost their creative spark

May you look around and witness the collective weariness that is weighing all of us down, artistic expression dampened by insecurity and unease, may you take just a moment to allow yourself to imagine wildly, beyond what's immediately in front of you, beyond a murky future, beyond the practical things you must do simply to get through the day, and may you feel the embers of inspiration still there, beneath the ashy mess, patiently waiting to be ignited the moment you're ready to light them again.

Amen

July 26, 2020

For those who could use a nudge

May these words be the first of many affirming nudges you notice today, whether the message that resonates most with you is "Keep going," "Please pause," "You're

amazing," "You're doing OK," or something
else, and may you marvel at how, if you
pay attention, affirming nudges often
come in truly unexpected places, some
words on social media, a call, a text, an
e-mail, a postcard, the random kindness
of a stranger, and while you're waiting for
the next nudge to come your way, may you
support the cycle, serving as the gentle
nudger for someone else who (like all of
us) is fervently longing to feel affirmed.

Amen

July 27, 2020

For those who are experiencing burnout

May you waste no more time wondering
if this feeling is valid and trust that your
body, your heart, and your mind know
best how to tell you to slow down, may
you actually listen, without shame or guilt,
assured that this is a natural part of a cycle,
one that requires you to actually believe
that no one, including you, can move at this
pace forever, and may you actually, right

now, make a plan for when you will rest,
before you forget this truth and disappear
into your hurried timeline again.

Amen

July 28, 2020

For those who got up on the wrong side of the bed

May you be honest with yourself and not
try to explain away this cloudy mood, may
you avoid the encounters that can wait
until tomorrow, may you do at least one
thing that you want to do, even if it doesn't
lift this heaviness, may you remind yourself
that this is temporary, that there are other
sides to the bed, other chances, and other
mornings, and may these bright, lasting
truths in the offing get you through the
transitory gray of today.

Amen

July 29, 2020

For those who are struggling to pull it together

May you look around and see how unraveled we all are, how the perfect stitches and seams of normalcy are merely mirages, how reality mostly comprises awkward burps and hiccups, clumsy starts and stops, and may you stop striving for an immediately perfect tapestry and instead patiently wade through the clutter, letting go of the threads that no longer matter and lovingly regathering the threads that do.

Amen

July 30, 2020

For those who are feeling particularly sensitive

May you handle yourself with care, accepting that you are the only one who knows your most tender places, that you are the only one who knows your deepest triggers, that you are the only one who knows best how to hold yourself, may you feel comfortable telling those who need to hear it that today is one of those days, and may your honesty be the invitation that moves them to adjust their approach, to listen to their own fragility, or simply to let you be.

Amen

July 31, 2020

For those who are fearing the loss of unemployment benefits

May you see how many of us are sitting in the same boat, hoping that this stress and debt don't engulf us, may you gain some small comfort in knowing that the collective cry of a people cannot be ignored forever, and may our demands for dignity dig into the hearts of the powerful, reminding them that this need is never simply about economic stabilization but always about human stabilization, that this fight is never simply about saving money but always about saving lives.

Amen

August 1, 2020

For those who need to unplug

May you remember that the art of
unplugging does not merely urge you to
turn off your screens but also invites you
to intentionally interrupt your typical
habits, silencing the noise for a while,
pursuing practices of quiet in your head
and in your heart, trusting that the world
will keep moving, even without your own
constant motion, while you take a moment
to recover from dizzying busy-ness and
regain some equilibrium for yourself.

Amen

August 2, 2020

For those who are having trouble keeping up

May you step back and look at all you do,
and may you have patience with yourself,
remembering that these past five months
have forced us into new ways of working,
new ways of organizing, entirely new
ways of simply being, and may your

leniency for your own slowness allow
you to also embody a bit more patience
for everyone around you, assured that
an honest, intentional pace for all is far
more sustainable and effective than an
unnecessarily rushed urgency.

Amen

August 3, 2020

For those who need a miracle

May you marvel at the facts that the sun
rose this morning and that you woke up,
remembering that these everyday things
were once thought of as mysterious
wonders to celebrate, and may you reframe
the mundanity of your day to call you to
awe, not in a saccharine dismissal of the
very real disappointment and suffering
of the world, but in an activating move
to remind yourself and everyone that, if
miracles like sunrises and awakenings
continue to occur, we just might be able
to conjure even more possibilities just by
paying attention.

Amen

August 4, 2020

For those who are feeling stuck

May you stop trying to force a huge change
and settle right now for a small one, may
you seek one connection who can help
you to soundboard just one complicated
task, may you offer the same help for your
connection, and may this mutual exercise
open up your tunnel vision a bit, expanding
the prophetic simplicity of the landscape
before you, showing far clearer paths
around the roadblocks than you'd dared to
imagine on your own.

Amen

August 5, 2020

For those who are numbed by the news

May you never hide from the realities
around you, but may you feel your body
telling you when it is time for a different
approach, may you see not only the
suffering occurring a block away, a state
away, an ocean away, but also the stories

of those who are responding, rebuilding, recreating in the wake of destruction, and may these helpers model how you might also offer your own gifts, especially once your nerves are sparking again and you can contribute more than despair.

Amen

For Lebanon, following a massive explosion in the port area of Beirut

May you feel the focused energy of the world holding you in solidarity and love, and as you enter this period of national mourning, may you sustain your collective strength to comfort the grieving, remember the lost, heal the injured, re-create what has been ripped apart, and demand continued accountability and change from the government, especially as the media move on, making it easier and easier for the powerful and for the rest of the world to lose this necessary focus.

Amen

August 7, 2020

For those who are feeling anxious

May you hear the hum of your worry and appreciate it for what it is, your body and mind keeping you engaged with both your own needs and with the needs of those around you, may you separate the helpful sounds from the useless noise, and may you find a certain freedom in thanking all of the racket, listening to the voices that keep you motivated for what can be addressed today, and sending the voices that drown out that motivation on their way.

Amen

August 8, 2020

For those who are feeling lost

May you realize that you've been here before, that you know this place, that you have felt hopelessly adrift in this very spot and still regularly found a way back out, may these familiar memories prompt you to rediscover paths that have freed you, regain survival skills that have saved you, and retrieve traveling partners who have journeyed with you, and by seeking these trusted trails, tools, and companions, may you also start to find yourself again.

Amen

August 9, 2020

For those who feel like they've tried everything

May you pause your panicked grasping for answers and resolve for now simply to ask good questions, realizing that the absence of quick fixes actually draws us into deeper creativity and that none of our old tricks are working anymore (which isn't necessarily a bad thing), may you recognize how awkwardly everyone is discerning new methods, and may you settle right now for committing to this collective research and development phase, as we all modestly rediscover who we can be.

Amen

August 10, 2020

For those who are heading back to school

May you listen to your gut as you make difficult decisions, may you not be afraid to demand safety and seek solidarity, may you speak up and step out as uncertainty abounds, may you hold institutions accountable to their promises of security, and may you remember that your life is more important than political posturing, that our future is more important than rushed solutions, and that a passion for education calls us to integrity, honesty, and collective health above all else.

Amen

August 11, 2020

For caretakers

May you gain strength from the gratefulness surrounding you, not only from those whom you immediately nurture, but from all of us who make up this society, a collection of hurting souls who are in even deeper need of patient protection than ever, may you have patience for your own waves of neediness and impatience, and when those waves do come, may the consistent heart you have modeled for so many prepare us to offer patient care for you, until you regain the patience and strength you so readily and regularly offer.

Amen

August 12, 2020

For those who are seeking balance

May you remember that balancing acts are dynamic experiences, not tricks that can ever be perfected, may you choose today to think of "balance" as a verb, instead of a noun, not a stagnant place you need to end up, but a vital becoming in which you are constantly engaged, may you find a certain peace within this motion, an activating calm that comes only from intentional, authentic movement, and may you realize that you've been balancing all along.

Amen

August 13, 2020

For those who are experiencing growing pains

May you marvel at the continuing education that life can be, may you remember that muscles atrophy unless they are exercised, that minds shrink unless they are challenged, and may you surround yourself not only with wise teachers but also with fellow students who are willing to join you in stretching, expanding, sweating, commiserating, and facing the satisfying burn of never-ending learning.

Amen

August 14, 2020

For the United States Postal Service

May you be honored as the essential public institution that you are, even as you are abused by the powerful as a politicized pawn, may your workers be surrounded by gratitude and safety, may your services be supported and celebrated, and as you continue to commit to delivering through snow, rain, heat, and gloom of night, may we all commit to protecting you from greed, dismissal, manipulation, and lack of insight.

Amen

August 15, 2020

For freelancers

May you find confidence in the fact that you know how to survive in a place of uncertainty, that even in a time of crisis you have honed tools, skills, expertise, and passion that still thrive, and if opportunities temporarily become scarily scarce, may your creativity know no bounds, may you unearth unexpected connections to nurture, may you discover rejuvenation in slowing down, and may aid, understanding, and solidarity sustain you, until your ample gifts are back in ample demand.

Amen

August 16, 2020

For those who are experiencing more solitude than usual

May you fall in love with yourself again,
not forcing happiness, but digging
for the deep joy that can come only
during moments spent alone, may you
acknowledge spikes of lonely fear, but may
you also set intentions for how you might
choose to plan, instead of panicking, how
you might choose to create a connection
with yourself instead of coming apart at
the seams, and may you remember that
you are the one who knows yourself best,
and that you're well worth getting to know
even better.

Amen

August 17, 2020

For those who are being forced to grieve in unfamiliar ways

May you be gently rocked by compassion
as we all continue to discover how best to
hold one another, may you find meaningful

ways to connect spiritually to the loved
ones you can't physically touch, may you
have generous conversation partners to
help you plan ways to mourn and celebrate
lives lived and lost, may you meet open
hearts who will listen to your honest pain,
and may we all nurture undying patience
for one another as we feel every individual
grief within this collective grief and seek
new healing together.

Amen

August 18, 2020

For those who are struggling to discuss politics with loved ones

May you remember that true love does
not equal silence or avoidance or even
acquiescence, may you ask questions that
call hardened hearts into self-reflection,
may you converse with a confidence
that allows you to listen to fear without
legitimizing it, to hear hate without
validating it, and may your love for
those most oppressed by our society's
systems model possibility for those you

love who have yet to step outside their own privileges and assumptions but who still might learn by witnessing your own continuing journey.

Amen

For those who have a shorter fuse than usual

May you listen to the jagged spikes of your own annoyance, acknowledging that you must be patient with yourself if you're going to be patient with anyone else, may you separate the real from the imagined, remembering that we are all waking up in a world that was already maddening even without our current added layers of grief and fear, may you seek ways to choose kindness, may you step away when kindness just isn't possible, and may you find ways to be kind to your own ornery self until you can offer that kindness to others again.

Amen

August 20, 2020

For those who woke up completely frazzled

May you do what you can today, accepting the not-perfect, the not-inspired, the not-quite-up-to-your-usual-standard, may you find a certain beauty in your body's uncanny ability to know when you must move a bit more slowly than you'd like, when you must take breaks that fly in the face of your obsessive productivity, may you offer gratitude for the fact that you are alive, no matter how tiring that aliveness currently feels, and may you find rest where you can, especially tonight, as you prepare to try again tomorrow.

Amen

August 21, 2020

For those who keep getting in their own way

May you take time to interrogate intentionally that critical voice, may you separate what is generative self-reflection

from what is self-sabotaging noise, may
you secure creative collaborators who will
help with that separating, especially when
your own ability is drowned out by your
own chatter, and may you make a lively art
of daily proving your snarkiest inner critic
dead wrong.

Amen

August 22, 2020

For California, as wildfires burn

May solidarity and support surround you
even as you are engulfed in flames, smoke,
and fear, may your first responders be
cloaked in safety and strength, may your
growing networks of mutual aid offer
lifesaving resources in the wake of chaos,
and as you suffer unfathomable layers
of loss, may you work lovingly together
to heal the wounds inflicted on your
residents, nature, creatures, and systems, to
transform this devastation into re-creation,
and to ensure that all can rise again from
these ashes.

Amen

August 23, 2020

For those who could use a moment of peace

May you listen to that subtle yearning
within you, the voice you often impatiently
brush off, and realize that this voice is
calling you to seek a slightly different
course today, not anything major, not
anything earth-shaking, but a simple shift
in your timeline and, whether you are
overscheduled and needing to postpone
one stressful plan or underscheduled and
needing to reach out to make one loving
connection, may you do just one thing that
brings you comfort and quiet, for no other
reason than the truth that the still, small
voice within you is asking for it.

Amen

August 24, 2020

For Jacob Blake, seriously injured by police in Kenosha

May you feel the empathetic energy of so
many of us surrounding your wounded

body, may the medical professionals who tend to your injuries be steadfast as their care combines with your own resilience to save your life, may your children be supported by loving kindness as they suffer the trauma of seeing their father treated mercilessly by excessive, heartless force, and may your name not join the list of those murdered by police, but may your story trouble our hearts until we actually dismantle the systems we've built and create new, justice-fueled, lifesaving visions in their place.

Amen

August 25, 2020

For those who are seeking purpose

May you observe the hurting world around you, the overwhelming news, the painful stories, the deep and continuing needs of your community, and may you choose small steps over big despair, not daring to think that you'll save everyone and everything in one move (or even one hundred moves), but starting where your own natural gifts might be most helpful, a call, a donation, a volunteer shift, a grace-filled gesture, and may you allow yourself to be awed by the simple, the doable, the actionable options that are hovering right in front of you, aching to be embodied.

Amen

August 26, 2020

For those who can't find any time for self-care

May you invite yourself into a new way of thinking about sustainability, one in which taking intentional time to step away from the flow and nourish yourself is considered not an additional stressful nuisance but rather the true foundation of your continuing wellness, may you make one promise to yourself today that has nothing to do with what you have to get done and everything to do with what your body and soul need, and may you make a habit of believing that you are worth treating like much more than a productivity machine.

Amen

August 27, 2020

For those who are facing the effects of Hurricane Laura

May you be surrounded by safety, even as your homes, security, spirits, and lives are damaged, may winds diminish, may waters ebb, and even as electric power goes out, may human power ignite the strength of mutual aid, linking those in need to those who can help, buoying all in solidarity, until recovery, rebuilding, and re-creation can begin, and may this devastation erode the hardened hearts of those who deny our climate-change emergency, pushing us all to confront the damage we've done and commit to truly listening to the demands of our natural world's torrential sobs.

Amen

August 28, 2020

For Anthony Huber, killed at a protest in Kenosha

Thank you for your courageous life, for embodying conviction and solidarity,

for putting your body on the line to
protect your fellow justice-seekers, and
as we mourn your death and honor your
conviction, may we not simply valorize
your selfless act of heroism but instead
heed the clarion call for a deepening of our
own participation, our own confidence, our
own necessary commitment to pressuring
the moral arc of the universe, in whatever
huge and tiny ways we can, until it actually
bends toward justice.

Amen

August 29, 2020

For those whose empathy muscles are working overtime

May you realize that those sharp pains in
your gut and this dull ache in your body
are the results of your paying attention,
refusing to ignore the grief and need
around you, may the exertion of these
muscles build continuing strength, so that
even if the hurt doesn't go away, it becomes
a deep reminder that you are keeping
your humanity in shape, keeping your

own heart from hardening, pumping care and commitment through your veins, and connecting your own liberation to that of everyone around you, an often arduous, but ultimately life-giving exercise.

Amen

August 30, 2020

For those who are wondering what they have to offer

May you combine humility with confidence, acknowledging both that you don't have all the answers and that you do have some of the answers, may you deeply feel how connected you are to a network of folks who are in the same situation, some with answers you need, some with needs you can answer, may you not shy away from asking for help or from offering your own gifts, and may this balance of mutual aid remind you that we can all be essential workers, if we are modest enough to listen for the ways we can best be of use and brave enough to never hide on the sidelines.

Amen

August 31, 2020

For those who need to catch their breath

May you take a moment and appreciate this radical act that is keeping you alive, may you bring into your body the air that the world is offering, as varied and complicated as it is, and may you hold it in your lungs, cradling it gently, until your body tells you to push back out into the world the air you wish to offer, infused with your hope, your fear, your grief, your love, may you remember that this quiet revolution is always happening, even when you're not paying attention, and may this knowledge urge you to check in with it a bit more often.

Amen

September 1, 2020

For those who just need to make it through today

May you pull yourself back from looking
too far ahead, may you nudge yourself
away from the nagging regrets of the
past, may you appreciate that, yes, life is a
collection of days, but right now, you can
worry about only this one, the one into
which you have awoken, the one in which
your only true imperative is to take care of
yourself and, with what you have left over,
take care of those around you, and may you
remember that, yes, there is much urgent
work to be done but, if life is a collection
of days, this one might just be one of those
that you simply have to stomach until
tomorrow dips in and you awaken anew.

Amen

September 2, 2020

For those who are having restless nights

May you make an art of routine,
intentionally creating space for calm,
keeping screens away from your resting
place, sipping something warm as you
wind down, reading poetry that lulls you
into a peaceful state of gratitude, but may
you also acknowledge the fact that these
six months have completely confused our
cycles, keeping our bodies both exhausted
and alert at all the wrong times, and when
you do wake in the middle of your sleep,
may you choose not to chastise your body
and mind for refusing to rest, instead
thanking both for working, telling you that
everything is not OK, and may this practice
of listening to yourself without judgment
help you to forget the rest for a while,
while you get the rest you need.

Amen

September 3, 2020

For those who fear that they failed yesterday

May you re-awake today not only in body but also in spirit and feel new air fill your lungs, new ideas fill your mind, and new possibilities fill your heart, may you learn from and apologize for mistakes made, for opportunities missed, for connections severed, and may you remember that we are as good as the next self-reflective, transformative, reconciling step we take, no matter what steps lie behind us, that life is a continuous series of awakenings, schooling us each day in the practice of forgiving ourselves and giving it another go.

Amen

September 4, 2020

For those who are facing eviction

May you feel solidarity surround you as your life is interrupted by anxiety and uncertainty, may you hear the voices around you calling for those in power to never settle for half measures that delay the inevitable and avoid real action, and may you know that we will not stop or shut up until our government steps down from its privileged tower, admits that this is not a partisan, abstract issue but an immediate need demanding concrete, imaginative response, and actually embodies its call to protect the safety, security, and shelter that should surround every human being.

Amen

September 5, 2020

For those who thought they had it all figured out

May you breathe in uncertainty as the old, familiar, annoying companion it is, may you feel connected to the collective unease of everyone around you as we continue to stumble through each new day, and may you encounter empathetic conversation partners who will help you turn anxiety into action, disquiet into curiosity, mystery into wonder, as we bump up against

one another, each and all of us steadily
becoming who we are, even and especially
when we fear we've forgotten who we
want to be.

Amen

September 6, 2020

For those who feel like they've aged ten years in the last six months

May you be gentle with your creaky bones,
your clouded head, your shortened fuse,
allowing your own pains to fill your heart
with compassion for the other aching
souls around you, may you listen to your
exhaustion as a reminder to rest, reshape
your weariness as a gateway to tenderness,
reframe your worry as an invitation to
attention, and may you celebrate yourself
as a sage-in-training, your body, mind, and
spirit not only aging but also growing wiser
with each new lesson of each new day,
especially when each of those days feels
like a week.

Amen

September 7, 2020

For those who labor

May you find deep meaning in your work,
may you feel gratitude surround you, may
you consider your offerings of time, energy,
and talent large parts of an even larger
whole, mysterious and miraculous, shaping
the future, affected by every gift each of us
gives, and may we all commit to creating
a culture of appreciation, one in which
none are exploited, and all are not simply
employed but also affirmed and celebrated
as the essential contributors we are.

Amen

September 8, 2020

For those who are seeking a bit of hope

May you not simply grasp for some
slippery, saccharine, theoretical concept
and instead listen to the deepest parts of
you, the parts that remind you why you
go on, the parts where you hold images
of the people whose laughter brings

you uncontrollable joy, where you hold
memories of those who have worked and
fought so that you can live and thrive,
where you hold vibrant dreams of all you
have yet to do and be, and may you hear
yourself loud and clear, a being who is not
quite there yet, but who is paying such
close attention to the beauty of it all that
you can't help but look forward.

Amen

September 9, 2020

For those who fear too much solitude

May you remember that this state is
something far richer than simply being
alone or loneliness, far deeper than simple
quiet and far closer to actual quietude,
may you challenge yourself to be still
and know who you are, especially if that
thought frightens you, may you seek new
regions of your self, especially if the terrain
terrifies you, and when this silence seems
too scary, may you choose to dig even
further, curiously loving yourself in ways
you've never dared to attempt before, until

the continuing journey feels absolutely
irresistible.

Amen

September 10, 2020

For those who feel like they're drowning

May you not be afraid to name it, this
feeling of suffocation, this pressure
on your lungs and heart, may you look
around and see the sea of others, all of us
treading water, navigating governmental
lies, continuing disappointments, and
growing grief, may you realize that, if we're
all drowning together, we can also rise
together, float together, find shore together,
and may this knowledge propel you to
offer breath to those who need it, to accept
breath from those who offer it, all of us
sharing oxygen and accountability, until we
make it to the other side.

Amen

September 11, 2020

For those we remember

Thank you for the gifts of your existence,
for all you did while here and for all you've
left behind for us to celebrate, and as we
mourn your death and remember your
spirit, may your memory be a blessing
to our present and our future, may
your example nudge us toward deeper
knowledge of ourselves and one another,
and may our fierce love for your life call
us to a daily renewal of our communal
commitment to actualizing abundant life
for all.

Amen

September 12, 2020

For those who need a change

May you step out of the shadow of self-
doubt and seek the warmth of conversation
with those who will listen to your desires,
hear your fear, and reflect back to you
the excitement you might not be able
to conjure yourself, may you remember

that no one in all of history has ever done
anything, especially transform, without
help, and may you open your heart and
mind to the voice within and to the voices
who believe in you, until that chorus sings
you into new keys you feared were far out
of your range.

Amen

For those who feel themselves disappearing into cynicism

May you be honest about the struggle,
the daily weight that threatens to drag
us all down into the shadowy depths of
dismissive despair, but may you also reach
out beyond the weight, to those who are
turning struggle into practice, those who
are molding passion into action, those who
are reshaping horror into opportunities
to help, and while we all continue to
hold the heaviness, may we recommit
to shouldering it together, lifting and
shifting as necessary, adaptive, persistent

weightlifters learning new ways to
sincerely strengthen our collective hope.

Amen

September 14, 2020

For those who fear the future

May you not disappear into your own
inner, uncontrollable angst and instead
move your focus to the things you can
control, to the deep well of joy that
can absorb even your most worrisome
moments, to the people around you who
are both offering and seeking conversation,
solidarity, and tool-sharing, to the
opportunities that arise when we open
our hearts and minds to both naming and
responding to the realities in front of us,
and if you can make only one change today,
for yourself or for all, may you count it as
one victory bubble joining with all other
victory bubbles, fragile, yes, but keeping us
afloat and centered in the only moment to
which we can actually knowingly respond:
Now.

Amen

September 15, 2020

For those who are dizzy

May you stop spiraling for a second and
hold on to something steadfast, a trusted
confidant who listens without judgment,
a practice that never fails to bring you joy,
a memory of a moment when you were
surprised to see hope actually pay off,
may you feel solidarity with your fellow
spinners as we reel from news of horrors
and harm, of hate and unchecked power,
and as you cling to the things that have
never failed you, may you allow yourself
to be refueled and refreshed, reminded
of the reality that swirling is not the only
movement available, that stillness is always
findable, that you can hold on for as long as
you need before letting go again.

Amen

September 16, 2020

For those who are just being born into this broken world

May you feel the welcoming, nervous hum
of this imperfect place surround you, may
you be protected from pain and shielded
from sickness, may you feel loved even as
so many of us so often don't embody our
most loving selves, may you feel connected
even as so many of us so often choose
to disconnect, may you forgive us for
the messes we've made and lead us into
more imaginative, justice-minded, spirit-
fueled tomorrows, and as your heart gets
broken, again and again, may its healing
remind you that while this world can
often be terrible, it is also always beautiful,
especially with you in it.

Amen

September 17, 2020

For Dawn Wooten, ICE detention center nurse and whistleblower

May you feel surrounded by gratitude and
safety as we thank you for your courage
and you prepare for the backlash, may you
stand firm in your resolve to tell the truth,
to shed light on sick, shadowy practices, to
risk your own life in order to rehumanize
those who have been so dehumanized, and
even on days when your bravery dips, may
you always deeply know how lovingly you
have changed the world, how boldly you
have underlined our need to pay attention,
how valiantly you have modeled for us
all how to remain human amid systems
that threaten to strip us of our humanity,
how to amplify our voices amid the brutal
banality of evil that continues to feed on
our silence.

Amen

September 18, 2020

For those who fear speaking their truth

May you remember that your authentic voice is necessary, that you are not simply a receptacle for others' ideas, opinions, and anger but a living, breathing being with your own organic wisdom to offer, may you open your heart to listening for where you might learn and where you might teach, for that sweet spot where humility and honesty meet, and may you balance both with every word you utter, assured that this dynamic act will bring you clarity, so that you may bring clarity to those who need to hear it.

Amen

September 19, 2020

For Ruth Bader Ginsburg, Supreme Court justice

Thank you for your fierce and fabulous life, for the trails you blazed, for the commitment to truth you embodied, for

the defiance you offered your naysayers,
for the strength, breath, energy, and
spirit you diligently contributed to our
continuing fights for justice, and as you rest
in the power you have so vigilantly earned,
may we loudly grieve with your loved ones,
may we loudly celebrate your legacy, and
may we invite your beloved memory to
reignite the fires of our political passion,
to resurrect our belief that persistence can
win, to nudge our hearts into devoted gear
to vote, to strategize, to organize, and to
make you continually proud of who we all
can be when we put our deep mourning,
our deep admiration, and our deep
gratitude to work.

Amen

September 20, 2020

For those who are getting lost in the hopelessness of it all

May you honestly name your fear, and then
may you pursue the company of those who
are reframing their fear and reimagining
it into evolution, may you remember that

concretized hopelessness is a heavy luxury that does not deserve the added weight of our attention, and may you instead give your energy to the causes that reignite your creative fire, to the work that reshapes your worry into new ways forward, to the futures that make your heart flutter with possibility, and in seeking these justice-minded, just-out-of-reach visions, may you find your collaborators, your calling, and yourself again.

Amen

September 21, 2020

For those who are already missing summer

May you breathe in the chilly snap of the air and feel the crisp possibility of fall fill your body, may you allow your nagging fears of oncoming wintry hibernation, of shorter days, of darker nights, simply to be, not trying to push them aside but naming them as necessary visitors who can't be turned away and who just might have new visions to offer, may you wrap yourself

in a blanket of community and solitude,
two sides of the same warmth that will
continue to sustain you, and may you allow
this seasonal transition to rock you gently,
giving yourself time to shed the old, rest for
a bit, and prepare for the new, an essential
rhythm that nature is beautifully modeling
for you.

Amen

September 22, 2020

For those whose endurance is flagging

May you remember that, even as these
past six months have tried and trampled
our bodies, hearts, and minds, this is not
a test to beat, a race to win, or a contest
to master, may you realize that the true
takeaways of this time will be rooted in the
memories of how we cared for one another,
how we cared for ourselves, how we
listened, comforted, helped, and raised our
voices, all things you organically know how
to do, and when you are weary, may you
ask for what you need, and when you are

heartened, may you share what's getting
you through, and may the circular breath
of this synergy continually refuel our
collective energy for the long, loving haul.

Amen

September 23, 2020

For those who feel pulled in too many directions

May you stop and breathe, simply and
steadily, trusting that the world's spinning
does not rely on your spinning, that there
is a difference between what you feel
must get done and what actually must get
done, that there is a distinction between
necessity and noise, may you choose the
next thing that deserves your attention,
addressing it carefully and calmly, and
when you have reached a pausing place
with that thing, may you choose the next
thing, building a pattern of patience over
panic, depth over dithering, and may you
surprise yourself with how much can be

done when you realize that you don't have
to do it all.

Amen

September 24, 2020

For those who are mad as Hell

May you not lose yourself in this shadowed
valley between rage and grief but instead
observe how many of us are sweating in
this scorching desert with you, may you
never deny this inflamed feeling, but when
you feel yourself about to be consumed by
the heat, may you reach out to those who
are collectively blazing ways out of these
despairing depths, may you offer your
rage as a gift to these uprisings, listening
to those who can help you organize your
anger into action and focus your fear into
sustained attention, and may you not reach
for hope before you're ready, but may you
invite the communal striving for it to keep
you climbing out of the fire.

Amen

September 25, 2020

For those who need a little encouragement

May you take a sure step back and marvel
at all that you actually do, even when you
simultaneously feel too tightly wound
and trapped in directionless freefall, may
you find those around you who could also
use a boost and support them, fostering a
reciprocal culture of gratitude that comes
back to you like a love-fueled boomerang
every time, and may this rotation of mutual
support model how we could be, what
we could achieve, who we could become,
if all of us would both embody and offer
the encouragement we hope will come
our own way and have confidence in how
deeply necessary our own gifts are to this
sacred cycle.

Amen

September 26, 2020

For those who don't know where to put all their nervous energy

May you gather up these sparks that keep you so on edge and pour them all into your passions, may you reserve a bit for your own creativity and may you take the rest, reach out to those who are fighting for the change you wish to see, and ask how your spirit, commitment, and talents might best serve a larger cause, and even when you have found directions for this electric flow, may you continue to listen to your body as it tells you when to be still before you burn out, and may you marvel at how the connection of this voltage within you to the currents of collective transformation around you channels hope in ways never possible if you tried to contain it.

Amen

September 27, 2020

For those who don't know where they fit in

May you realize that we are all always
hovering somewhere between confidently
claiming our places in the world and
fearing that we have no home to call our
own, that none of us truly feels that we
fit in without fail, may you start with
what you do know, that you want to make
connection, just like most people around
you, may you move from there to outreach,
finding those whose openness starts to
give you a sense of belonging, may you
challenge yourself to speak up about the
things you care about and encourage
those who speak up to you, and may this
supportive act begin to build shared shelter
that is big enough to house all of us, each
taking our place and leaving room for
everyone else to find theirs.

Amen

September 28, 2020

For those who need to make an apology

May you seek that generative spot between
uncertainty and nerve, the tension between
nervously knowing that repair is needed
and knowing for certain that the lasting
authentic strength of a relationship rests
on how openly we can admit to falling
short and recommit to the long haul, may
you not force forgiveness or acceptance
but instead listen for how your offering
of amends is heard, and as you work to
rebuild trust, may you trust your own
growing creative ability to take the lessons
you are learning and slowly but surely
shape them into new ways forward.

Amen

September 29, 2020

For those who need to let go

May you pause your fevered attempts to
control, to please, to undertake and overdo,
and whether it's something or someone

that is fueling that fever, may you ask yourself the hard questions, interrogating whether or not you have done what you can, offered what you've got, reached the end of the effectiveness of your energy, and if you have, may you give yourself permission to pause, to breathe, to turn toward the things and people that nourish your strength, instead of sap it, and may you find a new kind of courageous serenity in knowing when to stop trying to change what cannot be changed and change yourself instead.

Amen

September 30, 2020

For those who are still reeling from last night, following the first 2020 presidential debate

May you allow yourself to ache, to be horrified, enraged, scared, and sad, but may you not lose yourself, your hope, or your own voice in the noise of it all, may your own spirit's need to be lifted inspire you to lift the spirits of those around you,

may your own scrambling for strategy
point you toward the organizers who can
help focus and sustain your energy, and
may your fear for the future bring you back
to the present, a place where you have
connections, resources, and multiple ways
to combine your horror, outrage, fear, and
grief, breathe your longing for new life into
them, and recommit to co-creating the
country that is aching to be born.

Amen

October 1, 2020

For those who need some quiet

May you not take yourself so seriously that
you feel you must constantly contribute
to the noise, may you trust that the
community can sustain itself while you
take some time for yourself, may you
step away and approach this moment
intentionally, turning off screens, devices,
the constant nagging voices in your head,
and whether you are able to do this for a
day, an hour, or even just a minute, may you
breathe in the calm you wish to encounter

in the world and breathe that calm back
out into a world that rarely admits that
it needs it, and may your moment of self-
care inspire a chain of care that transcends
the babble and lifts it into a new realm of
collective communication.

Amen

October 2, 2020

For those who can't believe that they've been wearing the same thing for days on end

May you be assured that you are far from
alone, that we are collectively marinating
in soiled shirts and only occasionally
wearing pants, may you listen to your
heart to hear whether you need to worry
about this current practice or whether it
is simply a side effect of our continuing
pandemic culture, may you commit to
appreciating the clothing options you
typically enjoy and questioning our
questionable materialistic obsessions,
and may you remember that, right now

and probably always, there are far more important things than staying fashionable.

Amen

October 3, 2020

For those who were already having difficulty focusing before adding the chaos of this past week

May you remember that your life is far larger than the glare of the fickle news cycle, may you deeply know that, beyond the outrage, the confusion, the gaslighting, and the shifting predictions, your work and the gifts you bring to it are essential, your health is essential, your care for yourself and others is essential, and even as the stories continue to unfurl, double back, drift away, distract, digress, and die, may you keep your mind set on what is most essential to you, pour your energy into everything and everyone you love, and continue to keep your heart's vision focused on those new horizons we are currently conjuring together.

Amen

October 4, 2020

For those who are struggling to keep up with all the times they've said "Yes"

May you give yourself permission to do what you can, rest when you must, and sometimes practice saying, "No," may you not think of your "No's" as failures but rather as deep breaths, refueling and sustaining all that you do when you say "Yes," may you remember that not every bit of drama needs your own noise, not every bit of urgency needs your own anxious offering, and may your breathing give you ample space to recognize where your precious moments of "Yes" will be most life-giving to all.

Amen

October 5, 2020

For those who just don't know what to believe anymore

May you remember that, beyond the gaslighting, beyond the equivocating,

beyond the trickery, there are truths
that transcend, truths that you know
deep in your soul, truths that you feel
deep in your heart, truths that you
actively embody every time you listen
for the still, small voice inside you, and
may you connect it to the voices within
those around you, stepping away from
narcissism and nationalism, questioning
your own assumptions and privileges, and
continually co-creating new ways for truth
to reveal itself and rise above the lies.

Amen

October 6, 2020

For those who are feeling cowardly

May you never think of your fear as
weakness but rather as a message from
your soul, calling you to take precautions
and discern reality from fantasy, to
welcome the wisdom and help of those
who empathize, to reach out to the most
vulnerable and offer your solidarity and
protection, and to reshape this feeling
into a recommitment to connection, to

community, to taking the frightening
things of this world and responding
with fierce compassion, demanding
accountability from those in power and
building foundations and systems that
never deny fear but also refuse to let it have
the final say.

Amen

October 7, 2020

For those who are holding their breath

May you let it go, breathing into the
present moment, creating a foundation to
support the future, whether it's the one for
which you are desperately hoping, the one
that you desperately fear, or something in
between, and even as you work and worry,
may you breathe into these next few weeks,
offering more breath when you've got it
to give, resting when you need to catch it
again, giving others the support they need
to do the same, trusting that this steady,
cooperative, in-and-out rhythm is actively

fueling the birth of a future in which we all can truly breathe freely.

Amen

October 8, 2020

For those who fear that their vote won't count

May you stay vigilant about voter suppression, outreach, registration, and turnout, but while you wait and worry about the numbers, may you also think of your own vote as a sacred spiritual offering, not simply one tiny piece within a vast system but a love-filled representation of the vastness of your own heart, a prayerful symbol of your continuing commitment to nudging this country into transformation, a hope-fueled vessel for the mark you wish to make, and as you cast your own vision into the sea of visions, may it open you up to an invigorating understanding of just how necessary your participation always is.

Amen

October 9, 2020

For those who are looking for a sign

May this collection of simple words guide
your focus toward all that you might be
taking for granted, the miraculous fact that
you woke up this morning, the awe-worthy
reality that your body, even with aches,
injuries, and illness, is still a complex
system of cooperation keeping you alive,
the inspiring truth that your breath is
both a gift you receive from the world and
a gift you pour back into it, and may the
attention you give these oft-overlooked
wonders keep you seeking, even when
you don't immediately see the everyday
revelations unfolding right in front of you.

Amen

October 10, 2020

For those who are having technical difficulties

May you breathe through this moment,
deeply assured that, just because a tech
connection is unstable doesn't mean that

your spiritual connections are unstable,
may you reach out to those who can
calmly lead you through solutions without
judgment or snark, may you have patience
for the seeming magic involved in getting
our mysterious devices back in working
order, and may you offer gratitude for how
often such complex little inventions really
do work and for how the commitment and
care beaming between you and your loved
ones are built to survive even the most
annoying interruptions.

Amen

October 11, 2020

For those who could stand to love themselves a bit more

May you remember that your worth never
depends on your always being right or
being greater than others or winning
some imaginary success game, may you
remember that the value of each human
being transcends these momentary and
made-up markers, may you fight the lies
convincing us that we are constantly

competing for scarce resources, and may
you instead embody abundance, digging
deep inside yourself, finding where you
hurt the most, pouring so much love into
that part that it spills over, spreading to
all the hurting people around you, and
perhaps even convincing them to do the
same every once in a while.

Amen

October 12, 2020

For Indigenous Peoples' Day

May this observance be not merely
symbolic but troublingly transformative,
may it call us to reject the colonialist
mythologies that have populated our most
popular history books, may it celebrate
the cultures and stories that our white
supremacist narratives have sought to
destroy and bury, may it push us toward
repair and relationship before forcing
reconciliation, may it demand more from
us, even and especially when we think
it's too much, and may we commit today
and every day to honestly owning up to

our past, authentically interrogating our present, and moving carefully into a future that we must earn in order to create.

Amen

October 13, 2020

For those who have way too much going on

May you call out this anxiety for what it is, a combination of both the real and the phony, made up of both very present needs that you must address and very needless noise that drowns them out, may you separate the immediate from the imaginary, finding freedom from the fantasies that convince you that you aren't equipped to achieve, and may you decide to do just one thing today that reminds you just how capable of calm you truly are, making your way forward one manageable step at a time, instead of fearing that you've got to finish the entire overwhelming journey right now.

Amen

October 14, 2020

For those who are dealing with a disappointment

May you feel what you need to feel,
allowing yourself to grieve and rant, not
denying the dreadful power of defeat,
but may you also look far beyond this
temporary setback, knowing that no blow
forever defines your future and that no
bummer completely characterizes who
you are, may you do something today that
reminds you of exactly who you are outside
this momentary, uncontrollable hiccup
and, when you feel up to it, may you do
the only two things that you actually have
control over: process and persevere.

Amen

October 15, 2020

For those who are feeling peevish

May you be honest with yourself, whether
you are seeking more understanding for
your own annoying habits, or whether
you are seeking ways to breathe through

encounters with others, may you not be afraid to admit that something is nagging at you, may you step back and assess where it hurts, where potential calm is getting overshadowed by present discord, and may you honor this authenticity by finding the difference between what is yours to take on and what is yours to get over, then give time to the former and give distance to the latter, until you've created enough space for yourself to move on.

Amen

October 16, 2020

For those who can't believe how long this has been going on

May you feel the incredulousness of so many join your own, each of us navigating our own fears, griefs, and continuing malaise, may you reach out and unite your own fear, grief, and malaise with that of those around you, creating a connection that doesn't deny these feelings but instead grounds them in supportive community, may you then move to gratitude for those

who are using their energy and expertise
to take us to the other side, then may
you move to something like hope, not a
sentimental fantasy but a small, undeniable
tickle that forms when we combine
community with gratitude and mix them
into that mysterious stuff that keeps us
motivated.

Amen

For those who wonder where God is in all of this

May you consider that this name we have
given to the unnameable, this concept we
have attached to an unknowable, ultimate
mystery is actually at work in ways far
larger and more real than some invented
being in the sky, may you celebrate those
who are striving to make certain that
the oppressed find liberation, that the
suppressed can vote, that the vulnerable
find health, and that the powerful stick
to their callings and empower us all to
embody the common good, may you find

your own ways to participate, and may
this be the activity in which you put your
faith, not lamenting the invisibility of a
stationary noun but lifting up an active
verb you feel living and breathing in every
spirited moment of justice-minded mutual
aid.

Amen

October 18, 2020

For those who worry too much

May you thank this anxiety for keeping
things lively and then ask exactly what it
needs from you, may you make the effort
to climb out of its shadow and hold each
individual piece of it in the light, may you
find conversation partners who will gently
nudge you to separate the things that can
be reshaped into action from the things
that unhelpfully immobilize you, and
may you breathe through this separation,
assured that there are things you can do,
once you've cut through the meaningless

mess and are focused on the moves waiting
to be made.

Amen

October 19, 2020

For those who are about to try something new

May you be filled with a galvanizing
combination of guts and grace, conjuring
both the strength to silence your inner
critical voice and the smarts to listen
instead to the outer validating voices
that believe in you even more than you
believe in yourself, may you remember
that everything you've ever tried has
been brand-new at some point, and may
these memories float you through each
inevitable moment of self-doubt, until your
uncertainty reshapes itself into courage.

Amen

October 20, 2020

For those who just aren't feeling up to it today

May you radiate abundant patience for yourself, knowing that your body, heart, and mind are giving you signals that you need, reminders that they require attention and care, may you look at your day ahead and pinpoint pockets of time that you might claim for quiet rest and solitude, and, if it's possible, may you claim the entire day, but even if that's not possible, may you be gentle with yourself, inviting everyone you encounter to be gentle not only with you but also with themselves, a radical reminder that they might easily forget without your model guiding them.

Amen

October 21, 2020

For the parents of the more than 545 children who were separated from them at the U.S. border and still can't be found

May you be reunited, against all odds,
in the face of extremely intentional evil,
and whether or not reunion is, at this
point, actually a possibility or just an
impossible fantasy, may the irreparable
harms this country has inflicted upon your
families sear into all of our memories and
hearts, pointing our attention toward our
complicity, drawing us toward deeper
discernment, demanding accountability
from our government, pushing us all
toward participation, education, and
repentance, until inhumanity is eradicated
from our systems, the lies of white
supremacy are dismantled, and the cruel,
closed border between this country and
its moral conscience is broken down and
reshaped into an open, inviting threshold.

Amen

October 22, 2020

For Pope Francis, following the announcement of his support for civil union protections for same-sex couples

May you take this moment, filled with celebration from those you have affirmed and backlash from those who still fear the future, and open yourself up to more moments, more modeling of how a human being can grow, transform, question assumptions, and actively choose to embody evolving spiritual leadership, may you take the energy you have, combine it with the gratitude being beamed your way, and ask yourself where else your voice is needed, who else could use your solidarity, and how else you can continue to employ your humble power to shake up institutionalized harm into new, prophetic possibility, an exercise we all can embody, if we set our hearts, minds, and spirits to it.

Amen

October 23, 2020

For those who cannot take any more lies

May you not lose yourself in the noise but
rather be a vivacious seeker and sharer
of veracity, connecting with those who
are doing the work to make certain that
untruths are uncovered and that facts are
uplifted, may you speak up when you hear
deadly nonsense, may you call out harmful
myths, may you question yourself just
enough to continually educate yourself,
lest you be caught up in unfounded
fabrications, and may you find continual
hope in community-minded conversations
that challenge you to actually embody the
truths you so wish would be obvious to all.

Amen

October 24, 2020

For those who are not doing OK

May you listen deeply to that buzzing
alarm inside you, whether it is disturbingly
loud or numbingly quiet, may you hear the

solidarity buzzing around you, a society full of people also wondering if they have the strength and energy to keep looking for joy amid the mess, may you reach out for help when your lows sink too low, may you reach out to offer help when you have extra to give, and may you allow yourself to be OK with not being OK, never forcing false happiness, seeking instead an active, daily equilibrium supported by honesty and outreach, each of us gently teaching one another how to keep hoping for hope.

Amen

October 25, 2020

For those who are missing touch

May you find creative ways to balance our current need for safety with our perennial need for connection, may you hold yourself as tightly as you wish to be held by others, may you love yourself as fiercely as you know you are loved by others, and may your spirit reach out across the distance to touch and be touched through kindness, through compassion, through empathy,

all amazingly renewable resources that
sustain the sacred, invisible threads that
unite us, no matter what physical space
might stretch between us.

Amen

October 26, 2020

For those who are hoping to change hearts and minds

May you remember to keep your inner
eye focused on your own energy, engaging
others when you have some to spare
and resting when you are depleted and
despairing, may you keep in close contact
with those who are in this work with you,
those who will remind you exactly why you
are doing this, especially when encounters
with opposition threaten to steal your
joyous commitment to justice, and may the
potential and possibility on which you so
rely keep you primed for transformation,
even and especially when conversation
feels sticky, stagnant, and far from simple.

Amen

October 27, 2020

For those who need to fume today

May you give yourself the permission
you require, knowing that the ground
feels shaky, the air feels thick, the future
feels scarily uncertain, and then may
you reconstitute this anger into action,
connecting with those who are also
transforming their rage into a radical
recommitment to love, trusting that
this sparking electric current presently
flowing through your body is simply
seeking redirection in order to refuel your
continued participation in our hopeful
revolution.

Amen

October 28, 2020

For Walter Wallace Jr., killed by police in Philadelphia

Thank you for the life you lived, for the
change you made, for the children you
raised and the legacy they will continue
to carry, and as we shout your name and

demand accountability from the violent
systems that stole you from your family,
may our cries reach the deepest depths of
this country's continuing racist sins, may
we learn to actually de-escalate instead of
depending on brute force, may this society
learn to actually care for those whose
lives need protection, may this society
actually learn to honor the value of Black
lives and defund and dismantle insidious
imperial power, and may we hold ourselves
responsible for creating a world that no
longer has need for hashtags and knows
true liberation for all.

Amen

October 29, 2020

For poll workers

May you be surrounded by safety and
gratitude, may you feel the warmth of
beaming smiles beneath our masks,
may you be protected from conflict and
violence, may you be buoyed by the pride
of taking selfless part in our collective
act of democracy, may your work be

celebrated by everyone you encounter,
and may your generosity of spirit, your
hopeful offering of time and energy, rub off
on the rest of this country, showing us all
how collaboration, interdependence, and
recommitment might just light the way to a
bright and beckoning future.

Amen

October 30, 2020

For those who are feeling discouraged and disconnected

May you step outside your own sinking
thoughts and see the generous systems
working around you, even in the midst
of grief, even in the midst of fear, helpers
helping, voters voting, phone bankers
calling, text bankers typing, organizers
organizing, volunteers giving what they
have to give, may you remember that this
teamwork is always available, uplifting,
and effective, no matter what temporary
defeats rain down, and may you breathe
into this collective circular breath an
interdependence that is calling us to

continually name it, recognize it, and
embody it, even when things don't seem as
dire as they do right now.

Amen

October 31, 2020

For the thin veil between life and death

May you open our hearts and minds to
sacred memory today, reminding us of
those who have come before us, those
whose spirits hover around us still, those
who will come after us and cherish the
gifts we will leave behind, may this opening
not be frightening but inspiring, telling
us stories of where we've been, who we
are, and what we can become, and may we
deeply know that this unfolding is always
available to us, no matter the day or season,
if we will simply stop, breathe, and pay
hopeful attention to more than our fear.

Amen

November 1, 2020

For those who are dreading Election Day

May you be gentle with yourself and with
everyone you encounter, knowing that we
are all carrying weight that we don't even
understand, that we are all simultaneously
fearing and trying to predict outcomes,
that we are all struggling to live in the
present moment while deeply needing
to do just that, may you contribute what
you can, step away when you must, trust
that what you have offered is enough,
encourage yourself and those around you
to breathe, and may the inspiring visions
of collaborative community that you see
happening right in front of you transform
your incapacitating angst into active hope
for a co-creative future that will stretch far
beyond the anxieties of this week.

Amen

November 2, 2020

For our collective breath

May you steady us in the present
moment, reminding us that we are part
of a movement that is always larger than
any one of us and still needs every one
of us, one that transcends victory or
defeat, one that has room for our rage,
our grief, and our joy, may your in-and-
out rhythms model ways for us to both
take responsibility and let go, ways for
us to both offer what we have to give
and welcome what others have to offer,
may you nudge us toward solidarity that
will buoy us and transform worry into
transformative possibility, and may you
give us hope that our participation and
cooperation are constantly contributing to
a future that has breath and hope to spare.

Amen

November 3, 2020

For our country

May this swell of enthusiasm last far
beyond this day, may this abundance of
energy, this hum of history-making, this
recommitment to collective liberation lift
and sustain us long past this moment, may
the love we pour into our votes radicalize
our hearts, reminding us that we can be
this ecstatic and involved every day of
our lives, if we will only hold ourselves
accountable to embodying this excitement
until all can actually feel the freedom we
so often want to celebrate, may the visions
of who we must be transform the failings
of who we have been, and may we allow
today's eager steps to propel us forward,
humbly assured that we are creating a new
way and a new country together.

Amen

November 4, 2020

For those who are waiting

May you allow yourself to grieve this
delay, but may you also remember that this
hold-up is assuring us that all voices will
be held up, that all votes will be counted,
that those who have diligently exercised
their right will have their contributions
acknowledged, may you reach out to those
you love and find some rest today, may you
do something that pulls you away from
screens and back into the beauty of your
everyday existence, and may you trust
that this liminal feeling will transform
into something else, that you have done
your hope-filled part for now, and that our
continuing collective work will be there to
pick back up soon, no matter what.

Amen

November 5, 2020

For those who are feeling a bit impatient

May you welcome this nervous energy,
shaping it into recommitment to the work
that will still need to be done, no matter
what the votes tell us, may you meditate
on the issues that matter most to you and
make plans for your next moves, may
you educate yourself on the issues you
know less intimately, finding ways that
you can support those who are fighting
the fights you don't regularly enter, may
you acknowledge the intersections of all
of these issues and struggles, may this
acknowledgment make you feel deeply
connected to everyone around you, and
may these connections give you hope,
perhaps a jittery, irritable, uncertain hope,
but hope all the same.

Amen

November 6, 2020

For Stacey Abrams and so many other Black leaders and organizers

Thank you for your fierce commitment to fighting for fair elections, combatting voter suppression, lifting every voice, and singing us into a future that so many in this country have yet to actively embody, and as we celebrate the countless payoffs of your tireless work, may the memories of past oppression push us to remember and not repeat history, may the realities of continuing oppression push us to further transform our hearts and expand our minds, and may the oncoming visions that you are conjuring through organization, outreach, and deep faith challenge us all to live up to the promises of the country that you are moving and loving into actual existence.

Amen

November 7, 2020

For those who are feeling tentatively hopeful

May you hold on to this growing sensation, may you hold on to yourself, and may you hold on to those around you, may you not scroll or search for reasons to diminish this growing confidence but rather seek humbly hopeful connection with those whose faith will further inspire your own, those whose commitment to both this anticipatory moment and to the continuing work that will surely follow both lift you higher and deeply ground you, may you listen to the voices that remind us all that there is still much to be done, and may this increasing buoyancy float us into our next steps, convincing us that we can achieve all aspirations together, if we will only remain as authentically enthusiastic and interested as we are starting to be right now.

Amen

November 8, 2020

For those who are ready

May you celebrate this regalvanizing step,
this rekindling of a flame you feared was
about to burn out, this resurrection of
a fight you feared was dying away, may
you hear the shouts of unfettered hope
filling the air, locally, nationally, globally,
may you breathe in this solidarity, may
you offer gratitude for those who have
worked tirelessly to keep faith alive, may
you remember that this is a first move, a
re-igniting, a resurrection that will require
your continuing faith, fire, breath, and
forward motion, and may you invite this
joy you feel to become the fuel that keeps
you lit, inspired, and committed to the true
freedom that is still many steps away, but
eagerly awaiting our arrival.

Amen

November 9, 2020

For those who are somewhat daunted by all the work we have yet to do

May you welcome this bit of overwhelm
and hear it calling you to radical honesty,
may you be invigorated by this authenticity,
putting it to hopeful work instead of
allowing it to work you into a passive
torpidity, may you listen to the voices
that have been telling the truth about this
country for years, may you invite their
stories to inspire the developing ways in
which you will participate, ways in which
you will nudge this society to do more, to
listen more, to be more, and may you add
your own conscious commitment to the
building narrative of who we are becoming,
assured that our collective imagination
needs your active encouragement in order
to expand.

Amen

November 10, 2020

For those who are worn out

May you pay attention to your body, to
your heart, to your mind, to your soul,
and realize how hard they have all been
working, worrying over elections, wearying
through a continuing global pandemic,
wavering between all of the other things
unique to your own individual life, may
you offer patience to yourself, making a
promise to rest, whether that can happen
today or whether it needs to happen on
a nearby day on your calendar, may you
remember that rest is not simply a way to
refuel your work but actually an integral
part of your work, and may you give
gratitude for the fact that you are not a
machine but a complicated collection of
soulful parts that know when it's time to
stop acting like a machine.

Amen

November 11, 2020

For those who are yo-yoing between elation and worry

May you explore this rhythm with
curiosity, learning the ups and downs, the
lifts and dips, trusting that the art of living
is honed not through perfecting happiness,
which is impossible, but rather through
studying your own habits, strengthening
your own muscles, and experimenting
with new steps that will help you to more
nimbly navigate both the highs and the
lows, may you observe how many of us
are also seeking this balance, may you
ask others about the approaches that are
aiding their own equilibrium, may you
step back and separate the moves that
are within your control from those that
are way beyond your control, and may
you give your energy only to the things
that nudge you toward the promises
of empowering joy, letting the nagging
lies of disempowering anxiety go dance
somewhere else.

Amen

November 12, 2020

For those who are longing to be inspired

May you pay closer, focused attention
today, collecting the tiny miracles that
surround you, those minuscule things you
so often take as givens, the undeniable fact
that your body woke up this morning and
that, even with its aches and pains, it is still
awake, the fact that there is collaboration
happening around you at every moment,
even through the quiet ways in which
eyes meet, language is shared, listening
occurs, and understanding is sought, the
fact that, whether or not there is a divine
deistic pulse beneath it all, we are creating
collective divinity through our mundane,
quotidian connections, and may these
radically simple reminders nudge you
toward new ways to actively embody the
inspiration you wish to find.

Amen

November 13, 2020

For those who are itching for something new

May you remember that transformation doesn't always come in gigantic, earth-shaking waves but often in the form of tiny, almost imperceptible shifts, may you listen not only to your heart's deepest desires but also to those longings that feel too small, too silly, too insignificant to mention, may you commit to exploring one of those wishes today, may you tell someone about your plan, just to engender some extra accountability, and may you find fun in welcoming change a step at a time, allowing minor evolution, instead of being constantly crushed by the major overwhelm of enormity.

Amen

November 14, 2020

For those who can't stop looking at the news

May you remember that there is a
difference between being informed and
being incapacitated, may you absorb only
as much as ignites your recommitment
and may you turn away from the screens
and the stories when overwhelm seeps in,
trusting that you can take a break without
causing the world to break further, may
you dig more deeply into the hearts of the
humans around you, may you read the tales
told by the molting trees, the whispers
in the winds, the resilience of an Earth
that has seen it all before, and may you
then come back to the needs of this weary
world restored and renewed, ready to offer
yourself to living, breathing change, rather
than lose yourself in breath-stealing noise.

Amen

November 15, 2020

For those who just can't seem to find their stride

May you shower yourself with patience, acknowledging the time warp that is engulfing us all, one in which days slog by, feeling like weeks, and weeks flash by, feeling like days, may you remember that this combination of malaise and mania is presently our collective rhythm, may this knowledge make you feel less alone and alarmed and more forgiving of others' curious quirkiness, may you stop for a moment to re-steady your breath and recalibrate your heartbeat, and may you realize that both are comforting constants that are keeping you alive, rhythm-keepers to which you can always return, no matter how uncommonly inconsistent we all currently commonly feel.

Amen

November 16, 2020

For those who are definitely not looking forward to another period of sheltering-in-place

May you remember that, even though this feels interminable, this is not forever, may you give gratitude for all the alternate ways that we have to hold one another, even as their powers pale in comparison to in-person pleasures, may you reshape your fear of a current lack of freedom into a looking forward to future freedom, may you send hopes for strength and safety to those whose vocations afford them no option to stay inside, may you feel the potential of what we can do together if we will all cooperate, commiserate, and commit to protecting the most vulnerable among us, and may we all simply work from the place we are to get to the place we so desperately want to be.

Amen

November 17, 2020

For Nicaragua, Honduras, and all who are suffering the effects of hurricanes Eta and Iota

May you find safety and security, even as you are surrounded by winds that seem stronger than you are and waters that threaten to drown out your homes and hopes, may you receive the aid and solidarity you need in order to rebuild in the wake of destruction, may the hearts of those who can help remain moved and alert, even as our erratic news cycle alerts move on, and may this loss of life and calm urge us all to deepen our commitment to fighting for climate justice, not only for our future but also for a very present present that is acting out and crying out for all of us to truly change.

Amen

November 18, 2020

For those who don't know where to start with this praying thing

May you stop and gift yourself five minutes, may you bring your attention to your own body and give gratitude for the fact that it both tells you where it hurts and still keeps miraculously working as best it can with what it has and where you are, may you extend this gratitude to those familiar souls around you who are, just like you, most often doing the best they can with what they have and where they are, may you then extend this gratitude to those you don't know and may never meet but who also are most often doing the best they can with what they have and where they are, may you recognize how this expansion of gratitude connects you to a steady stream of goodness and good enough–ness, even in the midst of present pain, and may this simple truth be prayer enough for today.

Amen

November 19, 2020

For parents, guardians, and educators

May you breathe through these continuing
waves of uncertainty and stress, knowing
deeply that you are not alone, even as your
temper threatens to run away from you,
even as your inner voices convince you
that you are failing at every turn, may you
internalize the simple wonder of what you
are doing, teaching and raising our future
while you continue to be taught and raised
by all that life throws at you, may you step
back when you fear that you might lash out
at others or at yourself, and may you re-
ground yourself in the assurance that, even
while you are learning how to do this, you
are also actually doing it.

Amen

November 20, 2020

For students

May you be gentle with yourself,
acknowledging that school can already be

a slog, even without a global pandemic's keeping you glued to a screen and basically grounded, may you find fun in paying more attention to the subjects that ignite your imagination, and may you have patience for yourself when your attention wanders from the subjects that don't, may you remember that you are learning, every day, even outside the formal classroom, and may you study this moment with curiosity and generosity, approaching the possibilities in front of you like a difficult math problem needing more time, an obtuse poem needing more focus, a piece of music needing more practice, a test for which you are actually far more prepared than you fear.

Amen

November 21, 2020

For trans, gender noncomforming, and nonbinary folks

May you deeply know that, even as Trans Awareness Week ends and Trans Day of Remembrance and Resilience passes,

more and more of us are waking up, more
and more of us are remembering with
and honoring you, and as society both
exoticizes and harms your bodies, as the
mainstream media quickly move past your
stories and struggles, may you also deeply
know that a growing chorus of us are
committing and recommitting to speaking
up, calling out, and fighting like heaven
with you, every week, every day, every
moment, to make sure that you are not only
our brilliant future but also seen, valued,
celebrated, and protected now, here, in our
slowly but steadily queering present.

Amen

November 22, 2020

For those who wish they were preparing to see family in person this week

May you acknowledge this disappointment
for exactly what it is, a bitter bummer
felt deeply in your bones, adding one
more layer of letdown to nearly a year of
compromise, loss, and isolation, may you

not deny any of your sadness, but may
you decide to not allow it to be the whole
story, may you commit to doing at least
one thing this holiday season that feels
familiar, giving you a taste of times past,
and one thing that is brand-new, launching
you out of a comfort zone that has fizzled
for now and rocketing you into unfamiliar
territory that nudges you to create fresh
and unexpected traditions, and may this
balance between the out-of-reach old and
the just-dawning different be the spot
where you find some surprisingly sweet
celebration for yourself.

Amen

November 23, 2020

For those who feel like they're just spinning their wheels

May you focus on only simple things today,
nothing fancy or complicated, nothing
inauthentic or saccharine, may you not
force peace, may you not force calm, may
you not force change, may you be honest
with yourself and others about what is

possible today, even if that is just getting through it to another day, may you take some solace in the knowledge that so many around you are also just making it through today and the truth that honesty about this fact is the first step toward collective and personal movement, and may you be OK with your moves being minuscule today, until their gathering momentum slowly propels you into forward motion, maybe tomorrow.

Amen

November 24, 2020

For those who want to feel more grateful

May you take a moment, right now, no need to wait, it's just a moment, and think of just one person, no more than one for now, who has never given up on you, who has trusted you to never give up on them, who has kept you honest and been honest with you, who has seen you messy and been messy in front of you, may you focus your attention on how sacred a connection

this is, one that rarely requires gratitude
but one for which you are thankful anyway
and every day, and if you think of more
people and have more moments to spare,
go for it, but may you also be content with
this single, simple swell of appreciation
that's stirring inside you right now.

Amen

November 25, 2020

For those who are debating whether they will travel for the holidays

May you listen to the voice inside you
that is calling you to cautious questioning,
knowing that you are not inventing threats,
appreciating that there are expert voices
that are informing us on the compromises
we need to make, may you weigh the
pressures you feel and not avoid difficult
conversations with those you love, those
you wish to protect, those you so wish to
hug, may you dig deep to discover what
this season really means to you, and in that
digging may you tap into the true kernel of
your traditions, the beating heart of your

holidays, and may you make your decision from that place, where celebration is not tied to a physical space or a moment in time but is rather an abiding, available constant, no matter where you end up.

Amen

November 26, 2020

For the continuing education of our country about Thanksgiving

May we humbly interrogate the myths that have pervaded our history lessons for too long, may we offer back stolen breath to the real stories that have been intentionally buried, the true tales that tell of the invasive violence of settler colonialism, of Christian supremacy, of white supremacy, may we offer gratitude for the self-reflection toward which this rediscovering points us, for the repentance and reparations it requires of us, for the unending honesty it urges us to embody, may we learn new languages, those of relationship over domination, of honesty over self-preserving fantasy, and may we

actively transform ourselves into a society
for which all can actually authentically
give thanks.

Amen

November 27, 2020

For those who can't stand waiting

May you trust this nagging period
as a time of foundation-building
nourishment, sculpting you, through both
disappointment and tentative hope, into
the kind of being who will be equipped to
handle what's coming, and when it does
come, may you reshape antsy anticipation
into present preparation, pouring
your humming energy into reinforcing
relationships with yourself and with
others, co-creating a structure that can
hold impatience in all of its attention-
seeking angst but certainly doesn't let it
take up all the space, and may you dwell
here, confident that the future will visit,
but also content with all you're doing to be
able to simply settle where you are for now.

Amen

November 28, 2020

For those who could use a boost of confidence

May you never force manufactured
bravery and instead remember that no
one in the history of this world has ever
achieved anything fully free of doubt, may
this reminder quiet the needless noise
telling you that you're not enough, still
the self-defeating vibrations in your body,
heart, and mind, and comfort you with
the simple truth that genuine courage is
a combination of listening and learning,
much more than it is brazenly acting out,
may you realize how much listening and
learning you already do every day, may you
recommit to listening and learning even
more today, and may this revelation and
recalibration give your spirit the gentle
jumpstart it needs to dare you to believe in
your own authentically unassuming power.

Amen

November 29, 2020

For those who could stand to slow down a bit

May you pause, step out of your hurried timeline, and ask yourself why and to where you're even rushing, may you stop looking forward for a moment and instead look inward, inviting a hush, instead of your usual haste, challenging yourself to reflect, instead of randomly running, and when others question your pace, as they probably will, since capitalism is designed to make us mistake intentional lulls for laziness, may you be open about exactly what you're doing, steadily daring others to realize for themselves that the art of taking breaks isn't the opposite of getting things done but rather the only sustainable way that anything actually ends up getting done.

Amen

November 30, 2020

For those who are having to make tough decisions

May you remember that you have
been here before, feeling nervous and
inadequate, taking on something much
like this, even if the details were slightly
different, even if the painful present always
feels far more searing than the vaguely
recalled past, may you remember that,
back then, you reached within and beyond
yourself, ultimately trusting both your
own intuition and the collective wisdom
surrounding you, may this learned strength
flow to you now, assuring you that there
will be a time when you look back on
even this current predicament and marvel
at how resourceful and resilient you've
become, and may this bit of time-traveling
remind you that, right this very moment,
you are just as resourceful and resilient as
you hope to remember you were.

Amen

December 1, 2020

For those we remember, those we celebrate, and those we support on World AIDS Day

May the fierce witness of your lives echo in our hearts, today and all days, beyond grief and fear, beyond government lies and societal dismissal, beyond stigma and stagnation, may your fabulosity know no bounds, may your visionary rage grip our imaginations, may your survival, whether in body or spirit, urge us to do more, to be more, to act up more, until education and dedication lead us, at long last, to zero new cases, to just systems and abundant resources, and to honest healing and bold hope worthy of your vibrant, living memory.

Amen

December 2, 2020

For those who see a light at the end of the tunnel

May you allow this glow to lead you
forward, but may you also not immediately
dismiss the dark, may you continue to feel
what the shadows are doing to and for
you, may you understand more and more
deeply and celebrate how different you
will be once you reach the other side, may
you continue to move carefully, listening
for the soft sounds of those around you,
those who are traveling right by your side,
even when you can't quite see one another,
and may we all remember the new ways
of being that this collective journey has
asked us to embody, especially when the
gorgeous glare of a new day welcomes us
to forget.

Amen

December 3, 2020

For those who feel like they're teetering on the edge of a cliff

May you embrace the acrobatic urgency of unease, appreciating the truth that even those who appear to be perfectly holding themselves together are just as uncertain as you are, especially in these uncertain times, may you find footing in the fact that you have both deeply rooted resources and intelligence inside yourself on which to draw and deeply rooted community outside yourself on which to lean, and when you feel like the constant push and pull is about to shove you over the brink, may this balance between drawing on your own gifts and leaning on the gifts of others help you to hover, until you feel grounded again.

Amen

December 4, 2020

For those who could completely zone out for an entire year

May you surround yourself with
supporters who understand the power of
pausing to reclaim your right to relax, and
even if twelve months might be a bit long
and inconvenient, may you be assured
that twelve minutes or even twelve hours
might just do the trick, and no matter what
responsibilities might be screaming at you
from your to-do list, may you turn in, may
you stretch out, may you doze off, may
you dream on, may you escape annoying
urgency, and may you be ferociously quiet,
especially when the annoying noise of your
own head tries desperately to alert you to
things that really, truly, sincerely can wait.

Amen

December 5, 2020

For Middle Collegiate Church, as its congregation recovers from a devastating fire

May you feel embraced by the admiration, prayers, and solidarity of the millions of us who are constantly blessed by your actively courageous faith, and as you grieve the damage inflicted on your physical sanctuary, may the fierce spirit of sanctuary that you so powerfully embody every day give you strength right now, may your unstoppable message of revolutionary love continue to rise and heal this broken world, and as you rise and heal from this moment of overwhelming brokenness, may you be nourished by a constant flow of spiritual, emotional, and financial support, rebuilding a new hope and a renewed home for all that you have been, all that you are, and all that you will be.

Amen

December 6, 2020

For those who need time to mourn

May you respect your own process and
refuse to hurry yourself, especially when
the world tries to move you along, may
you weep, knowing that weeping is action,
not inaction, may your own cries give
permission to those who have not yet given
themselves permission to cry, and may
your present shedding of tears offer you
watershed moments that will lead you into
the future, once you are ready to follow in
their wake.

Amen

December 7, 2020

For those who need some time to themselves

May you close your doors for just a
moment and focus your full attention on
your own need for restorative solitude,
may you stop trying to force constant
engagement with others, may you trust
that your own soul knows when it has

been run ragged and that you know how to
heal it if you will only stop and tend to its
ornery creaking, may you remember that
the only sustainable way you can continue
to love others generously is by first
generously loving yourself, and once you've
reclaimed that self and reinforced your
own foundation, may you open up again,
welcoming others back into the orbit of the
renewed sanctuary that you've become.

Amen

December 8, 2020

For the Pfizer-BioNTech vaccine

May you find your way to those most in
need, to our essential and medical workers,
to our elders, to the most vulnerable among
us, to forgotten populations who cannot
effectively distance, may your potent
promises not convince us that we are yet
safe but remind us to stay ever-vigilant in
our own protective practices, and as we
keep you cold enough to remain effective,
may the hope carried inside you warm our
hearts with the glow of an approaching

light at the end of this long, but love-filled, tunnel.

Amen

December 9, 2020

For the Supreme Court of the United States, following its refusal to overturn Pennsylvania's election results

May you rejoice in this rare moment, one in which you all, with one brief sentence, despite the pressures and partisanship, dismissed the dangerously ridiculous as dangerously ridiculous, and may this unified action continue to show you how to listen to one another more deeply, to see one another more clearly, to regularly and humbly step outside your own silos to seek commonsense connection, until you build a chain of just actions and just decisions that just might shift this country toward good for good.

Amen

December 10, 2020

For Human Rights Day

May this 72nd anniversary of the signing of
the Universal Declaration of Human Rights
be not just a memory of a moment or a
remembrance of disembodied promises
but rather a reminder of universal truths,
that every person has inalienable rights,
that we must always acknowledge our
interconnectedness, both in the midst
of a global tragedy and far beyond it,
that equity, nondiscrimination, and
sustainability must be core principles of
a post-pandemic world, and as we look to
the future, may we recognize both how
far we have come and how far we have to
go, so that we will not be too daunted by
the continuing work but rather reinspired
to truly live into these weighty words we
celebrate.

Amen

December 11, 2020

For those who are trying to figure out what really matters to them

May you listen as earnestly to the things that bring you uncontainable joy as you do to the things that keep you unbelievably stressed, may you connect with conversation partners who remind you of your purpose and your gifts, may you steer toward the opportunities awaiting you at those promising points where your deepest passions meet inviting possibilities and veer away from those paths that are merely distracting dead ends, and may you trust the moments when your soul or those who know your soul tell you to let something stressful go, certain that there are many places where your energy, time, attention, and commitment will be put to much more powerfully joy-sustaining use.

Amen

December 12, 2020

For our democracy

May you continue to withstand the
relentless attacks pelting your fragile
power, may those who seek to undermine
your integrity be regularly, resoundingly
rebuked, may more and more of us realize
that the violence of corruption may wound
but collective honesty always has the final
word, and may each government decision
to uphold your virtue inspire each of us
to recommit ourselves to securing new
possibilities for the most vulnerable among
us, those who still have yet to taste the
fullness of your promises.

Amen

December 13, 2020

For Charley Pride, musician, who
died of coronavirus complications

Thank you for the open-hearted spirit
of your musicality, for the collaborative
generosity of your creativity, for the sturdy
steadiness of your leadership, and as we

celebrate your achievements and mourn
your passing, may we listen to the yearning
in your songs and commit to continuing
your radical legacy, making you proud of
the ways we tend and extend the trails you
have so brilliantly blazed.

Amen

December 14, 2020

For the Electoral College

May you listen to your better angels,
instead of entertaining the nefarious
noise surrounding you, may you live into
your duty to represent the will of those
you represent, instead of giving in to
the pressure of democracy-demolishing
dubiousness, and until a more just system
is secured, one in which the maneuverings
of the elite can no longer erase the
achievements of the oppressed, may you
take seriously the honor you are still
afforded today and do right by a country
that still has yet to do right by all.

Amen

December 15, 2020

For Asbury United Methodist Church and Metropolitan AME Church, following the vandalization of their buildings and Black Lives Matter signs

May you feel the committed solidarity of so many surround you, calling for an end to the myths of white supremacy and for the eradication of racial violence, may your pain be felt by all, pushing us to interrogate the large and small ways in which our individual and collective complacency perpetuates such myths and such violent acts, and until we actually root out this rot, until our systems actually convey the truth that Black lives matter, may we atone for this continuing history through action, through speaking up, moving beyond our facile calls for reconciliation, and actually living into the transformation that real reparation truly requires.

Amen

December 16, 2020

For those who are preparing for a nor'easter

May your bellies be full, your homes
secure, and your bodies and souls warm,
may you find ways to offer sustenance,
shelter, and warmth to those who are
not as lucky as you might be, may you
hunker down, but may you also reach
out, acknowledging the fact that, with
the continuing effects of these past
nine months swirling around us, we are
all more vulnerable to the chill of this
oncoming storm, and as we seek the heat of
connection and community, may our social
support systems also have a fire lit beneath
them, urging those with power to fight
for sustainable sustenance, shelter, and
warmth for all.

Amen

December 17, 2020

For those who are detained and have been participating in the hunger strike inside the Bergen County jail

May you feel support surround you, permeating the walls that confine you, reminding you of the multitudes who are fighting alongside you, and as we witness the power of your protest, may we all feel your hunger, your pain, your determination to dismantle the walls that stand between the cruel realities of this country's systems and the visions of who we must become, and may we all recommit to abolishing these dehumanizing barriers and building rehumanizing sanctuaries in their place, until all hungry souls need not strike but are instead free to taste the life-sustaining liberation that should be available to all.

Amen

December 18, 2020

For those who are feeling rushed

May you listen to the wintry call for
slowness, for reflection, even for
hibernation, may you feel how the chill
in the air demands a steadier breath, how
the ice on the ground demands a steadier
step, how the call to stay home demands
a steadier relationship with your own
solitude, may you make an art of stopping,
an art of waiting, an art of honing patience
and pause, and while you clear the way for
this steady creation, may you remember
that motion comes in many forms, even
and especially those that don't look like
movement at all.

Amen

December 19, 2020

For the Moderna vaccine

May your travel be swift, guiding you to
those most in need, to our essential and
medical workers, to our elders, to the
most vulnerable among us, to forgotten

populations who cannot effectively distance, may your potent promises not convince us that we are yet safe but remind us to stay ever-vigilant in our own protective practices, and as we offer gratitude to the multitudes who have funded, fought, and contributed their own time, talent, expertise, and bodies to your miraculous possibilities, may the hope carried inside you remind us all that we can create the miracles we so desperately hope to experience, if we will commit ourselves to caring for others as much as we hope to be cared for and loving our collective way out of the bleakness that tries to convince us that we are merely on our own.

Amen

December 20, 2020

For those who are dreading this week

May you not seek to bury this feeling but rather sit with and even transform it, may you be honest about how horrible this year

has been, how hollow the words "Merry,"
"Happy," and "Holiday" ring right now,
and until they ring true again, may you
not merely muddle through but rather
dig in to those things that don't depend
on temporary festivity but are rather so
constant and steady that they often get lost
in the partying, those things that continue,
especially when the tinsel has been pulled
out from under us and our usual traditions
fail, and may you open yourself to these
quiet gifts right now, trusting that they
are there, buried beneath both the merry
noise and the not-so-merry noise, holding
everything together with hope, especially
when we must be apart.

Amen

December 21, 2020

For the winter solstice

May you invite us to connect ourselves
again to the Earth, to the cosmos, to both
ancient history and continuing history, to
the ways in which our interdependence
used to guide our collective movements

and how it might again, if we will only
listen for its clear and obvious call, and as
we sit in the shadows, alone and together,
may we remind ourselves to not fear
the darkness, but instead feel it igniting
our inner lights, to not fear the cold, but
instead feel it kindling our inner warmth,
and to not fear this changing season but
instead know that its transition means that
change is also always possible for every
one of us.

Amen

December 22, 2020

For those who are not feeling relieved

May you raise your voice, connecting it to
that of so many others who are done with
denial and delay, who are sick and tired of
being pawns for the powerful and offered
offensive pittances, may our united voice
grow until it roars in a new reality, one
in which we care less about stimulus and
more about survival, where it is not enough
simply to be alive, unless all are helped

to thrive, and until these visions of how things truly can be become obvious to all, may those with open hearts and minds be elected, may those most marginalized be more and more represented, and may those who have hardened their hearts and closed their minds be ousted from office with echoing urgency, leaving our systems to be re-created by those who consider their power to be nothing less than a sacred call to collective care.

Amen

December 23, 2020

For those who are feeling blue

May you find some peace in knowing that you are not alone, that blue is the tint of this holiday season, no matter who or where you are, may you reach out to those around you, knowing that your authentic sharing of your own shades of color is also always an invitation for others to be more authentically in touch with their own, may you know that deep love undergirds these interactions, even when there is space

between us, may you know that deep joy
endures within us, even when happiness
feels out of reach, and may you know that
deep hope is on the horizon, especially
when we're being completely honest about
how far we feel from it.

Amen

For those who are trying to make this holiday nothing less than perfect

May you stop and remember that the
stories we constantly tell, the traditions we
most cherish, the images that echo loudest
in our hearts are often the ones birthed not
in perfection but in imperfect, authentic,
well-let's-just-get-through-this-together
love, when dinner burned, when the soloist
cracked on the high note, when that last
hidden present just couldn't be found,
and may you lean into the truth that true
celebration is not about fleeting, purely
picturesque moments, but rather the deep
work of making joy from the muck, making
peace from the mess, and finding hope in

the undeniable fact that we are not just marking time until next year, but making memories right now, right here, mucky and messy stories to add to the favorites we will tell for years to come.

Amen

December 25, 2020

For December 2021

May you be everything that we hope you will be, packed with physical family togetherness, stuffed with hugs and free of masks, as bright in real life as you are right now in our projected fantasies, and until you do come, may we continue to do everything in our collective and individual power to ensure that when you are unwrapped and revealed, as many of us as possible are there to greet you as the glorious gift you are, a possibility-filled future that we've not only been waiting for but actively creating together.

Amen

December 26, 2020

For those who just don't know what to do with themselves

May you breathe, may you be, may you settle, may you free yourself of made-up obligations and phantom nudges, may you snooze, may you dream, may you rest much more than it seems you should, and if you really must do something that feels productive, may you make a simple list of the things you will do when it's safe again to do most anything, trusting that you currently have no deeper calling than to do your part to make certain that, when the time is right, we all have the chance to get out our wishlists, compare hopeful notes, and know exactly where to go and what to do from there.

Amen

December 27, 2020

For those who are struggling to understand the heartlessness of some people

May you stop occupying yourself with
attempts to explain the inexplicable, may
you stop trying to find logical reasons for
illogical actions and inaction, may you
realize that there are simply some for
whom power, money, and self-deception
are the only comforts, and may you not lose
yourself in the hardness of these truths
but rather use this frightening moment
to recommit yourself to connecting
and organizing with those who see the
collective potential in power-sharing,
mutual aid, and reality-facing, and until the
representation in our government reflects
the best hearts we have to offer, may we
fight to create a society that forces no one
to struggle to understand indignity or to
live in dignity.

Amen

December 28, 2020

For those who just have nothing more to give right now

May you acknowledge that you've been
here before, that you have felt this empty
and unable, and may you remember that
the only thing that truly replenished
your energy, the only thing that properly
prepared you to offer yourself again, was
making the prudent decision to back down
and sit down, may you listen to your body's
aches, may you listen to your deep fatigue,
and may you remember that the world
needs not more self-sacrificing martyrs but
rather more authentic examples of self-
care who can teach us all how to be wholly
human, especially when we so badly want
to be superheroes.

Amen

December 29, 2020

For those who wish they were stronger

May you stop dreaming of being different
and take a good, generous look at who
you actually are, someone who is holding
it together, no matter how tenuously,
someone who is supporting others,
even if they can't see your panic behind
the scenes, someone who is waking
up each morning, taking each day as
it comes, listening for what is needed,
and responding as empathetically and
thoughtfully as possible (which is the
actual definition of "strength"), and once
you have realized just how much you are
actually doing, may you simply continue
to do it, reminding yourself that "being
strong" is not some far-off model of perfect
power but rather this thing, right here,
right now, that you have been doing, and
doing beautifully, all along.

Amen

December 30, 2020

For those who want to take care of everything

May you look at your own history and, basically, the history of the world and realize that no one, including you, has ever done anything completely solo, may you take comfort in the fact that the entire art of living is a collaborative exercise, not a solo act, and may you be content right now simply to do your part, offering the energy and expertise you have to give, receiving from others what they have to give, and having enough healthy humility to know that there is no need for you to take on the entire world when your own world is showing you just how much you can rely on it.

Amen

December 31, 2020

For this outgoing year

May your many lessons ring loudly in our hearts, and may the echoing not petrify us in the past but electrify us for the future, may your clear cries for interdependence and collective repentance continue to reshape our systems and our selves, reminding us that we are called to constantly care for one another, not only in the midst of emergency but also in every single hour of every single day, and as we move onward into the unknown, may we transform grief into commitment, fear into connection, and anger into obligation, not content to simply see what comes next but convinced and confident that we, together, are the stewards, the nurturers, and the co-creators of the new year we so desperately know we need.

Amen

January 1, 2021

For those who are embarking on a new beginning

May you sit in this first moment for far longer than is comfortable, feeling the heaviness of all that has come before but refusing to let it weigh you down, feeling the pull of all that is about to come but refusing to let it drag you forward just yet, may you allow this present threshold to present itself to you slowly, inviting you to remember that calm is as important as clambering, that peace is as powerful as progress, and when you do decide to move on, may you not forget to take this openness with you, assured that fresh starts can be available to you wherever you go, if you will only continue to carry the sense of possibility you feel right now, pause often enough to let these portals pop open where you need them most, and allow them to simply hold you until you're ready for the next step.

Amen

January 2, 2021

For those who are missing a lost loved one

May you feast on memories, giving yourself more space than your hurried timeline typically allows, may you remember that we are not only the attendants of our

own experiences but also the keepers
of one another's histories, that our own
lives become what they are only because
of the ways we interact and absorb our
encounters with others, may you have
patience for your own process, balancing
celebration and sadness, and may you
deeply know that this bittersweet feeling
that is engulfing you right now is proof that
you are not only human but that you are a
human who holds the offerings of others
just as lovingly as you hope your own are
held in return, and that this collaborative
story-stewarding is the most lasting way
that we keep ourselves and one another
alive.

Amen

January 3, 2021

For those who are pressuring themselves to address it all

May you reshape this unnecessary savior
energy that is boiling beneath your skin
and redirect it toward the only real duty
you actually have in the midst of this global

pandemic, covering your own contribution
to our collective survival, and when the
stress becomes too much, may you not
get dragged down again into the lie of
unchecked self-sacrifice, but may you
breathe into the freeing truth that there
will always be things that are within your
control and there will always be things that
are far outside your control, and may you
trust others to take care of their own parts
while you recommit to becoming an expert
only at your own.

Amen

January 4, 2021

For Black Voters Matter

May you feel the majority of a nation
celebrating your tireless dedication to
nurturing collective power, may you hear
the support of so many raising up your loud
and proud commitment to those whose
voices are so often dismissed and drowned
out, and as you keep your sights set on
unveiling the truth this Tuesday, may
you be assured of the growing gratitude

undergirding your devotion, reinvigorating democracy and making certain that its future lies in the hands of those who will never let its yet-to-be-realized promises die.

Amen

January 5, 2021

For Georgia, in preparation for its Senate runoff elections

May every single vote be easily cast and counted, may lines move swiftly, may all who set out to make their voices heard be welcomed and encouraged, overturning the embarrassing history of suppression and segregation that has marred your history, and may this picture of democracy in action become the model for a future free of racism and corruption, until all our established systems truly become the embodied reflections of our purported values.

Amen

January 6, 2021

For Rev. Dr. Raphael Warnock, senator-elect from the state of Georgia

May you bask in the galvanized energy
lifting you as you offer gratitude for all who
have paved this way before and beside you,
may you breathe, knowing that the work
that lies ahead will be difficult but that it
will be buoyed by the continuing dreams of
your ancestors and the co-creative visions
of partners who will walk with you, change
you, challenge you, and remind you of who
you are and why faithful service matters,
and even when the immediate glow of this
day dims and the weight feels too much
to bear, may you listen to the strong, still,
small voice that stays steadily lit within
you, pushing you to keep everyone who has
helped to bring you to this historic moment
as proud of you as they are right now for
many moments to come.

Amen

January 7, 2021

For this mess of a country, following the storming of the United States Capitol

May we pause to take a hard, honest look
at ourselves, may we not waste our time
claiming that what we are witnessing is
not who we are, and instead collectively
wonder what must be done if what we are
witnessing truly is who we are, may we
loudly name and negate the unchecked
white supremacy and toxic masculinity
that has been allowed to fester and rule
for centuries, may we stop hemming and
hawing about reaching across some fake
aisle and instead pour our energy into
creating undeniable hope for the most
oppressed among us in the face of fascistic
cynicism, and may we together recommit
today to not denying the parts we have
played in the problems but to reclaiming
the parts we can play in the solutions with
newly humble and vulnerable vigor.

Amen

January 8, 2021

For Jon Ossoff, senator-elect from the state of Georgia

May you not be daunted by the hard work that lies ahead but instead energized and elated by the truth that years of faithful work by countless dedicated individuals have led to this current hopeful moment, and as the glow of your celebration bears the shadow of a Capitol in chaos, may you remember that it is not only for the historically good days but also for the historically bad times like these that you have been trusted to lead, trusted to rise above, and trusted to trust that this is not only your mess to address but the responsibility of all of us who will continue to trust, lead, and rise with you.

Amen

January 9, 2021

For those who just can't seem to focus

May you be tender with yourself,
acknowledging that we are all currently
experiencing countless individual and
collective traumas, both the very obvious
and the completely unseen, may you
receive ample patience, both from yourself
and from others, when you fumble, delay,
rest, cancel, and reschedule, and may we
together learn how to honestly name and
heal harm, how to authentically restore
and repair, and how to truly slow down in
order to stay steady, especially when we
unfairly wish we could just move ourselves
right along.

Amen

January 10, 2021

For those who can't stop scrolling

May you remember that you not only
need but also deserve sabbath, rest,
and restoration, may you balance

doomscrolling with joyscrolling, and may
you sometimes simply close your heart off
to the glare, assured that regular and brief
turning away is necessary in order for you
to stay tuned in to the work that will still
be there when you turn back to it again.

Amen

January 11, 2021

For those who are feeling embarrassingly tense

May you not force yourself to bear an
ill-fitting brave face but instead wear
your anxiety honestly, inviting others
to encounter their own, may you speak
truthfully about the shadows, may you
share authentically about your own
questions, and may we together separate
the real from the invented, learning how
to hold one another through mystery,
supporting the most vulnerable among
us and connecting through our own
shakiness, especially when we would all
much rather appear solid and unshakeable.

Amen

January 12, 2021

For those who are clenching their jaws

May you check in with yourself and relax,
not as a means of ignoring the reality
around you or disappearing into fantasy
but as an act of simple self-preservation,
assured that staying aware of your body
and of the ways that fear and grief are
quietly manifesting within it will protect
you from having to deal with the loud
buildup later, may you stretch your joints
and your mind, may you open your mouth
and your heart, and may you trust that
gently massaging both your mandible and
your mental health might just give you a bit
of relief to keep you restored for the long
haul.

Amen

January 13, 2021

For Congress, as voting to impeach the 45th president begins

May you choose today to uplift accountability over forced unity, repentance over forced resolution, honesty over forced healing, justice over forced peace, may truth-telling overcome lie-entertaining, and may the long-delayed eradication of white supremacy from our systems make new strides, gain new spirit, and finally cure the festering canker at the core of this country's wounded, yearning soul.

Amen

January 14, 2021

For those who are overwhelmed by their inboxes

May you pause, may you breathe, may you acknowledge that you are attempting to work in the midst of constant global, national, and personal trauma, may you remember that every single bit of correspondence that is stressing you out right now was sent by someone who is also attempting to work in the midst of constant global, national, and personal trauma, may you choose to extend abundant grace to yourself and to them, and may you trust that this simple act is your most important job for the time being.

Amen

January 15, 2021

For those who are counting the days

May you channel this antsy energy into initiative, for yourself, for your community, for the continuing work we'll still have to do, even after next Wednesday, may you celebrate the oncoming horizon, may you keep calmly focused, even as we witness and experience our country's growing pains, and may you recommit yourself today to the days beyond, to a life defined by participation in our collective awakening, and to a long view that can hold both the happiness that is unfolding immediately before us and the imperatives

we must embody in order to keep our
future on course.

Amen

January 16, 2021

For those who could stand to do something nice for themselves

May you stop putting it off and simply
do it, may you make it small, especially
if planning for something larger will
keep you delaying, and may you make no
apologies, to yourself, to others, to the
world, for simply taking a moment to do
a version of what all of us need, whether
we've allowed ourselves to realize it yet or
not.

Amen

January 17, 2021

For those who are daring to dream

May you keep it up, sincerely, assured
that your most radical superpower is that
fragile spark you feel right now that is

nudging you toward a horizon that might
at times seem too far off but is far more
worthy of your energy than the despair
that keeps trying to obscure it.

Amen

January 18, 2021

For Rev. Dr. Martin Luther King Jr. Day

May we refuse to whitewash this day
and this legacy, may we recognize the
many ways we have decontextualized
and misused this man's words in order to
protect ourselves from the real work in
front of us, may we raise up the countless
names of those who have devoted
themselves to the cause of freedom,
individuals we might not proclaim and
revere but whose blood, sweat, and faith
have transformed our past and present,
may we give gratitude for generous
leadership and for community organizing,
and may this moment not be a hypocritical
holiday from reality but rather a continuing
call to dismantle the idolatrous lies of

white supremacy, to battle the blights of racism, classism, and brutality that course through this country's soul and systems, and to boldly and humbly interrogate our living history so that we all might finally live into a story of continuing collective liberation.

Amen

For those who want to change the world

May you remember that you are doing just that, even when you can't immediately see the shifts, may you connect with others who are open to learning from you and who can also teach you their own ways of sustaining themselves through what feel like agonizingly slow movements, and may you find at least one thing today that ignites your faith in the fact that we are entering a time of both foundation-rebuilding and foundation-shaking, a disorienting and re-orienting moment in which we will all need to keep reminding one another of the undeniably transformative parts we each are playing every single day.

Amen

January 20, 2021

For President Joseph R. Biden Jr. and Vice President Kamala Harris

May you enter this day with vigorous hope, may you each pause to check in with your body, may you quiet yourself, feeling the anticipatory beat of your heart, may you breathe deeply, allowing your lungs to fill with fresh air, may you look back at all of the people and passion that have brought you to this place, and may you look forward to the work that awaits you, but may you also allow yourself simply to be fully present here, now, at the threshold of infinite possibility, may you be surrounded by safety, may you be free of fear, and may you be willing to be charged, challenged, and changed by the honor you are receiving today, modeling for us all how to embody the promises of our democracy by acknowledging our interdependence and recommitting to the connections that will continue to charge, challenge, and change us all.

Amen

January 21, 2021

For Day Two

May we allow the complex feelings overtaking our bodies and souls simply to be, whether it's deep relief, continuing grief, rage for the work long derailed and delayed, hope for the work that beckons us forward into the future, or all of these things and every feeling in between, and as the glow of Day One dissipates into memory, may we not go too quickly, but may we also not go too slowly, and may we together learn the new rhythms of the rest of our lives, gaining back our grooves and nudging ourselves to try the new moves we've been avoiding for years.

Amen

January 22, 2021

For those who are feeling fatigued

May you remember that, no matter how solaced or celebratory we might feel right now, we have still all just experienced a national nightmare whose violence is tied to deep history and whose legacy will continue to haunt us, may you remember that we are still in the midst of a global pandemic whose continuing traumas are tied to corruption, delay, inequity, ineptitude, fear, lies, and loss, and may you listen to your heart, your lungs, your muscles and your joints when they all tell you that this is untenable, that exhaustion is a completely acceptable bodily response to this level of consistent stress, and that weariness is not weakness, just a remarkable tool we hold that tells us to slow down, to name our need, and to grant ourselves the grace and the rest we know we all still deserve.

Amen

January 23, 2021

For those who fear that we might become collectively complacent

May you commit today to being a voice that refuses to call for unity without accountability, a voice that demands interrogation of the normalcy that so many lazily say we need, a voice that sows tough, steady love for the vision of who we can become if we will only actively embody it, may you listen to voices that will strengthen your own when you grow hoarse, and may we regularly nudge ourselves and one another awake, especially during this time when our celebration can turn so quickly and easily into sleepiness.

Amen

January 24, 2021

For those who could use some grounding

May you pause and check in with the core of your being, that steady, quiet sense

inside you that reminds you of all the mess
you have made it through, all the wisdom
you have gained and now carry inside
your own heart, all the strength you have
acquired by simply continuing to live each
day honestly, and if your core seems shaky,
may you reach out to someone who knows
your journey, even if only a bit, and may
you ask them to offer you a bit of their own
steadiness for a moment, remembering
that groundedness is not an unshakeable
state to horde when you've got it and
lament when you've lost it, but rather a
dynamic experience that can and should
always be shared.

Amen

January 25, 2021

For those who need a wake-up call

May you remember that "normal" has
historically excluded, abused, exploited,
murdered, enslaved, tortured, and delayed,
and may you actively aim for "radical"
instead.

Amen

January 26, 2021

For our collective health

May we listen to the experts, may we ask questions when we have them and let our egos and assumptions fall away, may we choose faithful collaboration over alienating fear, and may we double up on protection, for ourselves and for one another, until our courteous commitment pays off and we can safely unmask again.

Amen

January 27, 2021

For those who are wondering whether there has actually been a peaceful transfer of power

May you stay alert and aware that, alongside the signing of executive actions and the tentative hope of promises being made, there is an ample nationalistic white supremacist force that remains empowered, emboldened, and active, both above and beneath the surface of our news cycle, and may your awareness not drive you to ineffective despair, but may it instead push you toward more collaborative work, deeper education and mutual aid, honest self-and-systemic critique, and abundant collective connections, which are our only truly hope-filled paths toward peaceful, powerful transformation.

Amen

January 28, 2021

For those who are fearful of the announced domestic white supremacist terrorism threats

May you do the only two things that most of us can do in response to this news, stay alert and informed, and may you re-channel the rest of your anxiety into extra energy for the things you actually can control, strengthening your relationships, organizing, exercising and nourishing your body, drinking enough water, breathing, and feeding your soul with all that brings you joy.

Amen

January 29, 2021

For Cicely Tyson, actress and legend

Thank you for your life-long modeling of
fierce grace and unwavering commitment
to your community, for the humor and
humanity you unfailingly brought to our
stages and screens, for the generous ways
you have encouraged generations to believe
that they are also exemplary, no matter
their level of fame, and just as the stories
you told and the characters you embodied
live on in our media, may the memory of
your near-century of love-filled life be an
unending blessing, inspiring lives and love
for centuries to come.

Amen

January 30, 2021

For our imaginations

May we remember that the only real
change that has ever truly happened
has sprung from daunting visions that
shook our status quos, dismantled the
supremacist empire lullabies of reason,

logic, and complacency, and completely transformed the death-and-scarcity-dealing norms that we once thought would always be givens into life-saving and life-giving possibilities.

Amen

January 31, 2021

For SOPHIE, music producer and performer

Thank you for the infectiously creative ways that you blasted through the boundaries placed on art and identity, for the genius and generosity you offered your trans community, for your consistent breaking of society's binary barriers that deeply deserve dismantling, and for gifting us the uncontainable beat of self-empowering, embodied spirituality that will keep us dancing into a future that is still becoming.

Amen

February 1, 2021

For Black History Month

May this be a time of celebration, education, and inspiration, and may this country also finally challenge itself to think far beyond the boundaries of set-aside months and safely packaged lesson plans, committing to fresh visions, reparative policies, new leadership, and radical actions, liberating continuing Black history from the present and pervasive shackles of white supremacist systems, violence, and ideologies, and nurturing freely thriving Black futures.

Amen

February 2, 2021

For those who are grateful for what they have but also feel the weight of these past nearly eleven months in their bodies

May you remember that we can and often must hold several things at the same time, that it is all right, and even necessary, to

acknowledge the bitter with the sweet and
the wearying with the wonderful, and may
you pay attention to the tension, stretching
your muscles and your mind, offering
yourself ample grace, trusting that the light
layers of patience that we offer ourselves
and each other right now are strong
enough to carry us through the heaviness.

Amen

February 3, 2021

For those who messed up yesterday

May you quiet the noise of your mind
and take a moment to reflect on what
happened, may you humbly apologize
to those who may have been harmed,
including yourself, may you be honest
about the fact that you will probably still
stumble today, even in ways you may
never realize, may you learn what you can,
not just the easy takeaways but also the
lessons that dig deeper into your soul and
transform you for good, and may you, of
course, try again.

Amen

February 4, 2021

For the U.S. House of Representatives, as they vote on the potential removal of Representative Marjorie Taylor Greene from her committee assignments

May wisdom visit your chambers, pushing you to recognize, name, and actually address the natural results of years, decades, centuries of rampant lies, conspiracies, and white supremacist nationalism, may you take your duty seriously, remembering that, above all, you are called to choose the side of life-giving justice, to expel ego-obsessed extremism, to dismantle deadly status quos, to repent for the ways in which this country fails to unshackle itself from its original and continuing sins, and to co-create policy that actively envisions and enables pathways that will liberate and challenge us into a new kind of freedom.

Amen

February 5, 2021

For the AstraZeneca vaccine

May your efficacy against viral variants
renew our hope for collective protection,
may you and all other medical miracles
find their way to the most vulnerable
among us, especially those most often
left out of our society's care and concern
and oppressed by our myopic and cruel
systems, and may you serve as not just
one more spirited step forward, but as a
sure sign of how creative we can be when
we work together to get to the other side
of this Hell and fight like Heaven to get
everyone there.

Amen

February 6, 2021

For those who are bored out of their skulls

May you acknowledge and accept the
needling influence of boredom, a loyal
companion who never fails to remind
you of your intrinsic need for action

and engagement, even if its effect most often feels more irritating than inspiring, and before you avert your attention and dissolve into your classically comforting distractions, may you allow this feeling to prod you, pointing you toward the abundant opportunities for unexpected creativity packed into this auspicious emptiness.

Amen

February 7, 2021

For those who are feeling a bit broken

May you remember that many of the optimistic clichés and metaphors you've heard that feel trite and saccharine in good times actually still contain grains of truth to which you can cling in these not-as-good times, may you reach out not only to those who have helped you to hold your own hurt before but also to those whom you have helped to hold their own, may you be reminded that you have not only been healed before, but that you have been

the healer whom others celebrate, and
may you find ample ways to imagine what
repair might look like, not forcing yourself
to rebuild too quickly but assured that the
blueprint is still emblazoned on your heart.

Amen

February 8, 2021

For Britney Spears, Janet Jackson, and so many other women

May you feel the collective support
flowing your way as this current reckoning
highlights your plights, may we interrogate
our society's sustained habit of placing
women on pedestals with plans to sacrifice
them to our own hungry need to criticize,
minimize, and demonize, and may we find
new ways to celebrate without idolizing,
not allowing this to be some momentary
trend that quickly dissipates but rather
a truly conscientious recommitment to
being better than we've been, to calling
out misogyny and calling ourselves to
accountability, and to replacing our deadly

devotion to devouring with freshly creative ways to consciously care for our artists.

Amen

February 9, 2021

For the U.S. Senate, as the second impeachment trial of the 45th president begins

May the perennial promises of truth, accountability, and justice ignite the hearts of all, today and far beyond today, may you not simply argue, but transform the argument, may you not simply condemn but dismantle in preparation to rebuild, may you embody your sacred calls not only to represent but to repent when necessary, and may you remember that you are unmaking and remaking a country with every honest move you make, with every veracious step you take, and whenever you stand up and speak out for all our sakes.

Amen

February 10, 2021

For those who woke up already exhausted

May you take a moment right now (don't put it off, really, right now, before the day hurries you into rushed resignation) to check in with your body and your breath and your being, may you be honest with yourself about what you are capable of doing today, may you list the things that must be done today (not the things you've convinced yourself must be done, but the actual, factual things that must be done), may you look at the landscape of your day and find ways to get those things done while also lovingly pacing yourself, and then may you decide to be OK with not getting anything else done (really, just let the desire to overdo it go), may you forgive yourself for being human, and may you do something we humans should really be very good at, though we most often will ourselves to forget: Rest.

Amen

February 11, 2021

For Myanmar, following the coup d'état that deposed its democratically elected leaders

May you feel the solidarity of so many surrounding you, may our collective energy inspire your strength and undergird your safety as you raise your collective voice, may justice and democracy surface and flourish, even as some in power seek to undermine and eradicate their potential, and may the world keep watch, not allowing our attention to be diverted by our distracted news cycle but rather steadily supporting you as you fight to embody and empower the true will of all of your people.

Amen

February 12, 2021

For U.S. Senate Republicans, in advance of the vote to acquit or convict the 45th president

May you listen far more deeply than you think is necessary, may you step outside your own fear and move into a wisdom that awaits you far beyond the walls of your own political maneuverings, and may your steely hearts and minds be softened, opened, and forever transformed by something that far transcends your party loyalty to your own version of the truth: The Truth.

Amen

February 13, 2021

For those who need some distance

May you remember that, even in the midst of continuing physical distancing, overcommunication can be an oppressive and insidious force, may you pay attention to your exhaustion, to your weary eyes and ringing ears and aching fingers, may you realize that there is such a thing as too much meeting, too much talking, too much listening, may you find the strength to ask for the space you need, and may you marvel at the grace you receive from others who couldn't yet bring themselves to ask for the same thing.

Amen

For love

May you be something more than commercialized, commodified sugar and spice, may you be a steady spiritual imperative that pushes us out of our comfort zones and calls us, again and again, to radical relationship, to deeper commitment to justice, accountability, honesty, repair, and transformation, may you be a constant that cannot be abused or manipulated, may you be a renewable resource that respects boundaries but refuses to erect false borders and walls, may you be a truth that every living being feels enveloping their souls, and may you

nudge us, faithfully and firmly, toward
horizons of community and care that we
haven't yet dared ourselves to imagine.

Amen

February 15, 2021

For those who need a holiday

May you find the strength, sustenance,
and support that will help you to not wait
for the specific slots designated in our
national calendar and instead take the time
you need, when you need it, how you need
to take it, assured that you don't need to
be observing something huge in order to
simply observe your soul's small calls for
regular self-care and simply heed them.

Amen

February 16, 2021

For those who need some help

May you ask for it, knowing that none of us
can actually, or at least always, read minds,
may you remember how much you have

offered to others when you had it to give,
and may you now humbly request a share
of the well of communal care you so often
and lovingly help to sustain.

Amen

February 17, 2021

For those who are having to draw boundaries

May you be assured that the assertion of
your own value, needs, and limits is an act
of love, for yourself and others, and may
you be so regularly in touch with these
things that you are continually able to set
your own limits without building walls,
to address bad behavior in good faith, and
to feel the deep, peace-filled sense of self-
worth that you hope all might eventually
feel.

Amen

February 18, 2021

For Texas, as it is engulfed in a devastating winter storm

May all who are cold and vulnerable
find warmth and safety, may all who are
isolated and disjointed find support and
connection, may all who are hungry find
nourishment and may all who are thirsty
find clean water, and as you wait for power
to be restored, may those in power hear
not only your cries but also the cries of our
heaving natural world as it desperately
reminds us that, in the face of such obvious
climate change, it is up to us to actually
change ourselves.

Amen

February 19, 2021

For those who are being too hard on themselves

May you pause your stagnating self-
criticism and bring your attention back
to the honest, activating truth, that you
are a miracle, really, someone who has

weathered grief and disappointment, who
has lifted others when they couldn't get
up, who woke up this morning, no matter
how weary, to try it all again, and if there
are apologies you should make today,
may you not run from them, if there are
recommitments you should make today,
may you move toward them, but no matter
what direction you follow, for goodness'
sake, may you never forget that you are a
creation in process, unfinished, of course
but, even in the midst of your agonizing,
messy progress, still never anything less
than a work of art.

Amen

February 20, 2021

For those who are feeling unsure of themselves

May you stop to listen closely to your gut,
not that queasy feeling in the pit of your
stomach but the wellspring of gumption
obscured by the gurgling, may you realize
that, buried beneath the lazy lies you've
told yourself about your own inadequacy,

awaits an explosion of poise that might be alarming but is also invigorating, and may you decide to let it erupt today, assured that you are far too humble to ever get too haughty and allowing yourself, even if just for one unsettling moment, to be gutsy enough to go for it.

Amen

February 21, 2021

For those who can't seem to stop

May you be honest with yourself about what you are sacrificing when you refuse to rest, may you realize that burnout is not only something that happens to you but also something that happens because of you, may you remember the radically restorative feeling that comes when you admit to yourself that very few things actually depend on your being constantly wound up, and may you find freedom in the fact that your own survival actually depends on your willingness to wind down.

Amen

For those who could use a little kindness

May you reach out to those who have tenderly helped you to get back up in the past, may you offer them a bit of tenderness right now and, in doing so, may you reflect the image of kindness you so wish to see and marvel as it is mirrored right back to you.

Amen

February 23, 2021

For those who are learning to say "No"

May you realize that thoughtful denial is not only a form of self-care but also a form of community care, may you remember that not all requests are urgent, not all demands are valid, not all panic and punishment is yours to take on, and as you live into your own life-giving dissent, may

it remind others that a current "No" is also
a loud "Yes" to the future.

Amen

February 24, 2021

For Lawrence Ferlinghetti, poet, artist, activist, and publisher

Thank you for your prophetic witness
to the insurgent power of poetry, for
the generous nurture you have given to
countless voices by quieting your own and
allowing them to rise, for the bright city
lights with which you have guided restless,
wandering seekers, and for continually
reminding us that words have power,
that symbols are ours to dismantle and
re-create, and that plentiful playfulness
is a necessary ingredient for a continuing
revolution.

Amen

February 25, 2021

For a country mourning more than 500,000 COVID-related deaths

May our grief and our anger inform us, but not overwhelm us, may our keening come in the form of commitment, and as we dig deep into the sadness of our hearts, may we also dig deep into the failings of our societal systems, interrogating inequity, holding ourselves accountable, and reshaping our rage into a fierce love that will fuel us to both never forget those we've lost and forge a future far brighter than the fires that currently engulf us.

Amen

February 26, 2021

For our collective stamina

May we be honest with ourselves about the fatigue, the burnout, the fear and grief of nearly a year come and gone, and may we also feel authentically connected to the interdependent web of work happening around us, through us, and for us, each of us offering expertise, whether it be in the forms that explicitly address the ongoing threats of this pandemic or in the simpler forms that quietly and lovingly offer care, creativity, and comfort, all of it activating hope in ways that are often invisible, but always invigorating.

Amen

February 27, 2021

For our minimum wage

May $15 per hour be only the first step on a pathway toward embodied economic justice, authentic equity, and lasting prophetic witness, may our next move be a complete overhaul of our approaches to valuing labor and humanity, and may we refuse to rest until all work and all people are supported in ways that not only vocally celebrate how they sustain our society but also actually sustain their lives.

Amen

February 28, 2021

For the Johson & Johnson vaccine

May your convenience and benefits find
their way to those who need them most,
to those who have been held back by our
inequitable systems and selfishness, and
may your promises multiply, reaching
every corner where safety and hope have
yet to take hold, blazing trails toward
wholeness and health, not only for the
well-connected, but for all.

Amen

March 1, 2021

For Women's History Month

May we celebrate the countless
contributions, inspiring movements, and
hard-won progress, looking back at where
we've been and looking forward to where
we have yet to go, but mostly looking
honestly at where we are, who has been left
out along the way, what voices have been
drowned out by the continuing violence of
misogyny and white supremacy, and how,

even in the midst of our appropriately loud rejoicing, we can also challenge ourselves to more authentically uplift all.

Amen

March 2, 2021

For those who are just trying to hold it all together

May you breathe into a practice of self-sustaining patience, acknowledging that, yes, there are always more tasks to be completed, always more relationships to be tended to, always more plans to complete, but also accepting the truths that, sometimes, things do fall apart, connections do suffer hiccups, arrangements do go awry, may you step away from the unhelpful noise that is telling you that every thread must be picked up immediately, and may you quietly choose one of them right now, may you carry that one lovingly, for as long as it needs, and then may you move to the next, gathering gracefully as you go.

Amen

March 3, 2021

For those who are regularly disappointing themselves

May you stop for a moment and remember that you are human, no more and no less, may you hold yourself accountable, but may you also simply hold yourself, may you open your heart and archive the information that will help you to change, may you offer yourself the forgiveness you need in order to keep going, and may you keep going.

Amen

March 4, 2021

For those who are coming to the end of something and the beginning of something else

May you refuse to rush this moment, may you find a way to ritualize what is happening, a way to appreciate where you've been and where you're going, may you take more time than feels appropriate, more time than you usually allow yourself, to reflect, and may you find a brief but powerful peace in this liminal space, a peace that is, of course, informed by all you've done and looks forward to all you'll do, but also a peace that can flourish only in these in-between times, a peace that is holy and wholly its own.

Amen

March 5, 2021

For those who need to take a breath and, for just a moment, simply be

May you.

Amen

March 6, 2021

For those who feel like they're wandering in the wilderness

May you pause your frantic tries to figure out how to get through this and instead center yourself by transforming your relationship with it, may feeling lost offer you more opportunities to ask for

directions, to try new paths, to share tools
and maps, and to move with more care,
and may you focus less on how far away
the other side seems and more on how
awesomely deep your knowledge of the
landscape is actually becoming.

Amen

March 7, 2021

For those who are about to explode

May you not dismiss this anger and rather
dive deep to touch the grief at its source,
may you pull it close, may you ask it what
it needs, may you investigate its causes
and seek conversation partners who will
listen rather than fix, and may you become
comfortable with combustion, choosing
to hear it, communicate with it, and trust
in its power to disrupt the you who you
thought you were and show you the you
you need to be.

Amen

March 8, 2021

For the family of George Perry Floyd Jr., as the trial of Derek Chauvin is delayed

May you feel the solidarity of so many surrounding you as you seek authentic accountability, may you find regular peace from the glare of media attention and re-traumatizing detail, may your love and memories sustain you through this latest trial in a long line of trials, and may justice come to light, igniting a future free of the violent lies of white supremacy and police brutality and fueled by the freeing fires of truth.

Amen

March 9, 2021

For those who see a glimmer of hope

May you not horde it from nor force it upon anyone else, may you instead listen to how this feeling is changing you, how it gives you breath you thought you'd lost and energy you thought you'd spent, and may

you treat it like the sacred resource that
it is, renewable if respected, generative if
tended to, and always available, even when
it becomes a bit less visible again.

Amen

March 10, 2021

For those who need even more relief

May you feel your cries supported by
the many voices demanding that those
in power thaw and reshape their frozen
hearts, may you find the mutual aid
connections that will nourish your body
and spirit in the meantime, and may we all
hold our social safety nets accountable to
their moral imperative to catch and hold
us all, especially those who so regularly fall
through the cracks in our consciences.

Amen

March 11, 2021

For the one-year anniversary of the World Health Organization's declaring COVID-19 a pandemic

May we balance grief with gratitude, refusing to ignore the very real hardships suffered and lives lost and choosing to give thanks for the ways we see that the gifts of interdependence have filled in the cracks caused by corruption and delay, and may we co-creatively sustain this authentic harmony, long after the media have moved on, long after our government wipes its hands and conscience, long after it would be convenient to forget what we have been called to do together, what we are actively doing together, and what we must forever continue doing together.

Amen

March 12, 2021

For those who need to do a bit more listening

May you not rush to answer, explain, or defend, may you remember that you don't always, or even ever, need to have an immediate fix, may you find the quiet core that keeps you nourished enough to feel worthy and open enough to be changed, and when you do respond, may you ground yourself in trust and be heard as deeply by others as you have just practiced yourself.

Amen

March 13, 2021

For the loved ones of Breonna Taylor, on the first anniversary of her murder

May you feel the collective energy of so many surround you, not a true comfort in the face of the enormity of your loss but still a growing groundswell demanding that change come, that the violence of white supremacy and police brutality be

abolished, and that names not simply be
said but actively remembered, until we
actually put our systems, our votes, our
money, our hearts, and our commitment
where our mouths are.

Amen

March 14, 2021

For those who are moving more slowly than usual

May you listen to your body, instead of
rushing it, may you still your mind, instead
of scolding it, and may you remember that
both often show you the pace at which you
should actually be moving, whether you
like it or not.

Amen

March 15, 2021

For those who are questioning themselves

May you quiet the critical voices inside
and outside you and decide to take them

seriously, but not personally, may you
remember that you shouldn't always
know the answers, as thinking that you do
keeps you closed off to curiosity, that you
shouldn't be fully grown, as that gives you
nowhere to go, that you shouldn't always
be right, as that is something of which
literally no one is capable, may you breathe
into the powerful truth of who you are
right now, someone who is always learning
from and teaching yourself at the same
time, and may you stay inquisitive enough
to keep doing both.

Amen

March 16, 2021

For queer folks, following the Vatican's reassertion that priests should not bless same-sex unions

May you remember that any church
which refuses to respect your life does not
deserve to affect your life, may you find
your faith in the chosen family that not
only affirms your existence but also loudly,
lovingly celebrates it, and may your spirit

be infused with the gospel truth that the
divine delights in every single moment
you dare to spend being unapologetically,
fabulously you.

Amen

March 17, 2021

For Asian communities, following the targeted, anti-Asian mass shootings at Atlanta-area spas

May you be buoyed by the outrage and
solidarity supporting you as you grieve loss
and violence that directly connect to this
nation's living legacy of white supremacist
lies, may you be surrounded by safety, and
may the racist rhetoric at the root of this
pain be continually called out by all until
its architecture is eradicated and overcome
with an embodied commitment to long-
avoided transformation.

Amen

March 18, 2021

For Deb Haaland, U.S. Secretary of the Interior

May this historic moment give you breath, inspiring you to speak out for the land and people most affected by our continuing legacies of colonizing greed, may you ground yourself in truth when you are questioned, may you center yourself with strength when you are challenged, and may we all lift up your voice, not only symbolically but also in very real ways that question our own assumptions, challenge our own consumption, and call us to an energetic transformation far more radical than our violent, lazy history has yet unearthed.

Amen

March 19, 2021

For sex workers

May you be deeply affirmed in your work and value, may you be safe from exploitation, trafficking, white supremacy,

misogyny, and violence, may you be
surrounded by a loving community that
is vocal and invites you to be vocal about
your worth, and may you be unfailingly
respected and celebrated, not in spite of
what you do but because of who you are.

Amen

March 20, 2021

For those who need a reminder or two or three

May you remember that you are doing
the best you can with the wisdom you've
acquired, the resources you have, and
the connections you've made, and if you
still don't feel that you are, may you take
a breath, be patient with yourself, and
commit to learning something new today,
to asking for something you need today, to
reaching out to someone today in the way
that you would like to be reached, and may
you be amazed by the wisdom, resources,
and connections that are right there in

front of you, just waiting for you to pay attention.

Amen

March 21, 2021

For the second day of spring

May you remember that, after the brash excitement of that first day, the radically quiet work of resurrection continues, not always named but always accessible, in the anxiously tentative buds, the embarrassingly ecstatic blossoms, the enduring, silent circle of blooming that is your life.

Amen

March 22, 2021

For those who just want to do the right thing

May you remember that there are both things within your control and things far outside your control, may you accept the fact that you are fallible, and, following a misstep, may you choose simply to make the next best move, and may you find freedom in tethering yourself to your own integrity, the most valuably renewable resource available to you when you feel emptied and unmoored.

Amen

March 23, 2021

For Boulder, Colorado, following the mass shooting at King Soopers supermarket

May you feel support encircle you as you grieve, may you feel solidarity surround you as your shock gives way to fear and anger, may we finally pay attention to how our idolatry is slaughtering us, how rampant guns combine to kill us all, and may we demand another way, a path that is possible if those in power will do more than just think and pray.

Amen

March 24, 2021

For those who are celebrating a tiny achievement

May you be as quiet or as loud about it as you desire, may you deeply know that no moment of success is too small to shout about, may you remember that it is the abundant energy packed inside even the smallest victories that sustains us through the times when larger triumphs feel far away, and may you find community who will remind you of the mammoth power of modest joys, especially when you dismiss your own as less mighty than they truly are.

Amen

Acknowledgments

My lucky life is filled with generous
people whose huge imprints are threaded
throughout these tiny prayers and
throughout everything I do. I am, before
anything else, a student and a seeker, and
my continuing education includes lessons
from the lives of countless others—writers,
thinkers, leaders, practitioners, makers,
those I have met and those I haven't—and
I humbly acknowledge that nothing in this
collection has been created in a vacuum.
I and these prayers are the products of
every influence I encounter, and the year
between March 2020 and March 2021
brought many new encounters, both with
immediate grief and with enduring models
of resilience, so accordingly, I lift up the
lives of those we have lost over these past

months, and I lift up those who dedicate
their lives to building collective liberation.

I offer specific gratitude to Richard
Morrison, Eric Newman, Angela Moody,
and all at Fordham University Press,
who shepherded this little collection to
publication with such encouragement
and care; to Pádraig Ó Tuama, whose
poetry gives me life and whose blessing
of a Foreword gives these prayers extra
breath; to the Reverend Elizabeth G.
Maxwell and Dr. Robert J. Rivera, whose
early reviews of these meditations were
integral parts of their transition from social
media posts to book form; to Graham
MacIndoe, whose cover photograph
is the perfect encapsulation of the
yearning spirit of these reflections; to my
professors at Fordham University and
Union Theological Seminary, who taught
me the power of combining attention,
intention, time, and quiet; to Mary Ann
and Frederic Brussat and all at *Spirituality
& Practice*, who created both an online
space for these offerings and a kind, warm
home at which to hone my voice; to my
multi-faith colleagues, who continue

to teach me the abundant potential of
simultaneously claiming my own tradition
while remaining open to a lifetime of
learning from other traditions, especially
Ezra Bookman, founder of *Ritualist*,
whose boundless creativity, nimble mind,
and infectious love of spontaneous ritual
regularly make my heart sing and whose
"A Ritual for When You're Trying to
Zoom with a Friend but the WiFi Sucks"
specifically inspired the Tiny Prayer for
October 10; to the organizers, activists,
and artists whose fierce commitment to
creation and justice inspires me to keep
going and to keep making; to Fred Rogers,
whose radically loving example challenges
me every day to become a better version
of myself and whose gentle nudge to
"always look for the helpers" specifically
inspired the Tiny Prayer for August 5;
to Octavia E. Butler, whose Earthseed
verses featured in her novels *Parable of
the Sower* and *Parable of the Talents* have
deeply nourished my own spirituality
and expanded my understanding of the
earth-shaking potential of liturgy; to all
who read, shared, questioned, challenged,

appreciated, recited, and co-created these
prayers as they were posted on social
media and whose engagement kept the
practice going; to anyone who has ever
generously corrected my mistakes and
assumptions and offered me the grace to
try again; to the staff and congregation
of Judson Memorial Church, who have
shaped me into who I am today, as a pastor
and as a human being, and who are some of
my favorite holy troublemakers, especially
Michelle Y. Thompson, whose voice and
vision are wonders to behold and who so
often galvanizes my own imagination; to
my feline familiars Cat Stevens and Little
Wonder and my canine familiar Carl
Thomas Dean, all of whom always know
the right moments to lie silently by my
side and comfort my anxious heart; to my
friends, who unfailingly forgive me and
help me to not forget who I am, especially
Jean Railla, whose gift of joyful enthusiasm
is its own brand of spiritual superpower,
and Isaac Oliver, who unofficially edits
my words and constantly brings me back
down to Earth with just the right balance
of critical sensitivity and sass; to my family,

especially Ann, Dave, Barb, David, Jordan, Christian, Bridget, and Bobby, whose love for me frequently saves my life and shows me God; and to my husband, Matt, whose quiet passion, inexhaustible curiosity, and ability to answer my constant questions with effortless wit and eternal patience make me fall for him daily, whose steadfast support is itself a perfect model of prayer, and who is the most faithful faith leader I know.

Micah Bucey serves as Minister at Judson
Memorial Church in Greenwich Village, a
congregation committed to curiously seeking
the intersections between expansive spirituality,
radical social justice, and uncensored creative
expression. A graduate of Fordham University
and Union Theological Seminary, Bucey has
also served as Multifaith Coordinator for the
New Sanctuary Coalition of New York City
and is a regular contributor to Spirituality
& Practice. In his time at Judson, Bucey
developed and continues to oversee "Judson
Arts," which has commissioned, presented,
produced, and promoted the creative output
of hundreds of poets, actors, playwrights,
composers, musicians, dancers, choreographers,
painters, photographers, sculptors, and many
others, upholding the belief that artists have
the potential to serve as society's modern-day
prophets. Learn more at micahbucey.com.